Your
BIBLE
QUESTIONS
Answered

Douglas A.
Jacoby

HARVEST HOUSE PUBLISHERS

EUGENE, OREGON

Unless otherwise indicated all Scripture quotations are from the Holy Bible, New International Version®, NIV®. Copyright © 1973, 1978, 1984 by Biblica, Inc.™ Used by permission of Zondervan. All rights reserved worldwide.

Verses marked NASB are from the New American Standard Bible®, © 1960, 1962, 1963, 1968, 1971, 1972, 1973, 1975, 1977, 1995 by The Lockman Foundation. Used by permission. (www.Lockman.org)

Verses marked HCSB are from the Holman Christian Standard Bible®, Copyright © 1999, 2000, 2002, 2003 by Holman Bible Publishers. Used by permission. Holman Christian Standard Bible®, Holman CSB®, and HCSB® are federally registered trademarks of Holman Bible Publishers.

Verses marked KJV are from the King James Version of the Bible.

Cover photo © iStockphoto / fstop123

Cover by Dugan Design Group, Bloomington, Minnesota

YOUR BIBLE QUESTIONS ANSWERED
Copyright © 2011 by Douglas A. Jacoby
Published by Harvest House Publishers
Eugene, Oregon 97402
www.harvesthousepublishers.com

Library of Congress Cataloging-in-Publication Data
Jacoby, Douglas A., 1959-
Your Bible questions answered / Douglas Jacoby.
   p. cm.
Includes index.
ISBN 978-0-7369-3074-1 (pbk.)
ISBN 978-0-7369-4122-8 (eBook)
1. Bible—Examinations, questions, etc. I. Title.
BS612.J33 2011
220.6'1—dc22
                                                    2010052596

All rights reserved. No part of this publication may be reproduced, stored in a retrieval system, or transmitted in any form or by any means—electronic, mechanical, digital, photocopy, recording, or any other—except for brief quotations in printed reviews, without the prior permission of the publisher.

Printed in the United States of America

11 12 13 14 15 16 17 18 19 / LB-NI / 10 9 8 7 6 5 4 3 2 1

Contents

Introduction

We are born inquisitive. God made us that way. At a young age we begin asking questions. As we mature, we grapple with issues and try to remain intellectually honest, especially in the absence of definitive answers. We are all tempted to jump at the ready answer. Certainty is comforting, but must be rooted in truth. Honesty may entail suspending judgment or admitting, "I don't know."

The questions in this book have been submitted by real people, seekers in Africa, Asia, the South Pacific, the Middle East, Europe, and the Americas. They asked, and I did my best to answer by telephone, e-mail, private appointment, and especially the Q&A sessions that follow my presentations worldwide. You may not always agree with my responses—I often even "disagree" with myself, changing my mind on various subjects as I mull over new information and other people's perspectives—but I am grateful that you are giving me an audience.

Of course we'll never have all the answers, and fortunately salvation isn't based on sophistication. "The secret things belong to the LORD our God, but the things revealed belong to us and to our children forever, that we may follow all the words of this law" (Deuteronomy 29:29). The search for truth must continue, for this is God's will (Matthew 7:7). Many of our discoveries enrich our faith, supply what is missing in the big picture, and equip us to help others who may be stuck in their own quest.

A crucial challenge in interpreting Scripture is determining whether the author was writing metaphorically or literally. In some cases, this is obvious. For example, if David found rest in the shadow of God's wings (Psalm 17:8), are we to believe God is a bird? Of course not. Or take Jeremiah 51:42-43, where the image of drought is superimposed on the image of flood. A literal meaning is obviously not intended. But the decision isn't always so easy. Are the days of creation in Genesis 1 literal 24-hour days? How many of the vibrant symbols in the book of Revelation are intended to be understood literally? In such cases, we do well to focus on the main point of the passage and not to be distracted by speculative positions.

The point of the search is not to be smarter or biblically savvier than everybody else. I remember a news item about a Bible-quoting contest that ended in murder. The loser was so incensed that he went home, grabbed a gun, and shot his opponent in the face. For many, it is unthinkable that they have got it wrong. Yet if we're mistaken, we need to admit it; if we gain new knowledge, we need to be thankful and humble. As the apostle Paul asked the Corinthians, "Who makes you different from anyone else? What do you have that you did not receive? And if you did receive it, why do you boast as though you did not?" (1 Corinthians 4:7).

As with individuals, so with churches. A fully biblical congregation won't say, "Don't ask, just believe!" or "We've always done it this way; why question it?" Ultimately, if the Bible is the authority, then the church is not, for the word of God trumps the word of man (1 Thessalonians 2:13). Groups are as unlikely to "arrive" as individuals are.

With this spirit of humility in mind, *Your Bible Questions Answered* makes a stab at a smattering of Bible questions that *can* be answered. To get the most out of this book, be sure to read the Scriptures cited in the questions. The answers assume you are familiar with them. Also, keep in mind that this volume is illustrative, not comprehensive. Some of the selections arise naturally from intriguing topics. Others are suggested by apparent contradictions or difficult passages. None of these, however, disproves or discredits the fundamental message of Scripture. At the end of the day, there are more answers than we have questions, for God has the answer to any and every question we could possibly put to him.

Douglas Jacoby
Marietta, Georgia
January 2011

Part 1

QUESTIONS ABOUT THE WHOLE BIBLE

1

General Questions About the Whole Bible

Where did the title *Holy Bible* come from, and what does it mean?

The word *Bible* does not appear anywhere in Scripture. Its source is the Greek word *biblion*, book, as in *bibliography*. As millions of people can testify from personal experience, the Bible is a library of 66 life-giving volumes.

The Bible is *holy* because it possesses a spiritually pure quality, not because we are to worship it. I like the acronym Basic Instructions Before Leaving Earth. Yet the purpose of this book is not just to relay information, but to bring about transformation. It is also holy because it connects us with the spiritual world, helping us to know God, as those willing to let the message penetrate soon find out.

What is Scripture?

Scripture is written communication from God to us, the word of God. This includes the sacred writings of the Old and New Testaments.

What is the layout of the Bible?

The books of the Old Testament are arranged in three sections in the Hebrew Bible: the Law, the Prophets, and the Writings. The books in Christian Bibles are the same, but the order is somewhat different. Malachi is the final book, though in Hebrew manuscripts, 1–2 Chronicles closes the canon.

In the Hebrew Bible, the Law is the first five books of our Old Testament. The Prophets include the former prophets (Joshua, Judges, Samuel, Kings) and the latter prophets (Isaiah, Jeremiah, Ezekiel, and the 12 minor prophets). The Writings consist of Psalms, Proverbs, Job, Song of Solomon, Ruth, Lamentations, Esther, Ecclesiastes, Daniel, Ezra–Nehemiah, and Chronicles.

Hebrew Bible	Christian Old Testament
Law Genesis–Deuteronomy	**Law** Genesis–Deuteronomy
Prophets 21 books	**History and Poetry** Joshua–Song of Solomon (17 books)
Writings 13 books	**The Prophets** Isaiah–Malachi (17 books)

The New Testament is laid out in four parts: Gospels, Acts, letters, and the Apocalypse, with 4, 1, 21, and 1 books in each section, respectively. In some ancient copies, the letters from James to Jude follow Acts; in others, Hebrews follows Romans. I have also inspected collections of the Gospels in which John came first or Mark preceded Matthew. But this hardly matters. It's not the order that is inspired, but the content.

When was the Bible written?

The Old Testament was written, for the most part, between 1000 BC and the late fifth century BC. Genesis 36:31 makes clear that the final version of Genesis, the first book, came sometime after the monarchy was established in Israel. (Saul was anointed as Israel's first king around 1050 BC.) The New Testament books were written between the 40s and 90s of the first century AD. Thus the entire Bible was written over a span of more than a millennium.

What are CE and BCE?

In an effort not to offend those who are uncomfortable with the claims of Christ, many in academic circles prefer the abbreviations CE (Common Era) and BCE (before the Common Era) over the traditional BC (before Christ) and AD (*Anno Domini*, Latin for "in the year of the Lord"). This book follows the traditional BC and AD convention. The era is presumably "common" because the entire world, even those who are not Christian, share a common calendar. So CE and BCE are the politically correct forms of AD and BC, especially since some world religions (such as Judaism and Islam) have their own calendars.

Yet regardless of whether the abbreviation is changed, the number for the current year (for example, 2011) is still based on the notion that more than 2000 years ago the most significant event of all history took place: Jesus Christ was born—God became flesh.

Has the Bible been changed? Isn't it a translation of a translation of a translation...?

Actually, modern translations are made from ancient copies. For example, the original Greek gospel of John was probably written at the end of the first century. Handwritten copies have survived from the second century onward. Today's English Bibles are translated directly from these ancient handwritten copies. So your Bible is a translation, but it's not a translation of a translation. Scholars work from the oldest manuscripts available in the original languages.

What do we mean when we say the Bible is inspired?

Inspired means more than just true. It also means more than "inspiring." Many documents are substantially true (invoices, magazine articles, police reports…) but do not qualify as Scripture. Others are uplifting or motivating (poems, sports journalism, war stories…), but this hardly requires divine inspiration. Inspiration refers to the *function* of revelation—its ability to guide, shape, and direct our lives toward God.

Second Timothy 3:16-17 states that all Scripture is both inspired and useful. But in what way? Some believers imagine Scripture somehow addresses every area of knowledge, human and divine. Every verse has a profound meaning, and nothing is incidental. The Bible contains comprehensive knowledge about history, physics, biology, psychology, and so forth. But this turns out to be a restrictive, flat theology; it presses Scripture into unnatural service, making it a mere textbook.

Some go even further and use the Bible as a sanctified Ouija board, flipping through its pages randomly in search of patterns, codes, or clues as to God's will for their lives. This misguided approach ignores the textured nature of God's word.

People sometimes confuse inspiration with a particular kind of interpretation. For example, those who interpret a passage literally may feel as if those who interpret the same passage metaphorically do not believe the passage is inspired. This is not necessarily true. Inspired Scripture communicates truth literally (for example, Jesus really will return to earth) as well as metaphorically (he probably won't have a metal sword sticking out of his mouth—Revelation 19:11-16).

Also, do minor discrepancies between the Bible and clear scientific or historical facts discredit the inspiration of the Bible? Not at all. Not one of these discrepancies affects the clear message of the Bible. And almost all of them are not really mistakes; they simply reflect the way people talked when the Bible was written. As for the nature of inspiration, one helpful viewpoint states that the Bible is "reliable in all that it genuinely affirms, and authoritative for guidance in doctrine and behavior" (the Lausanne Covenant). For more information on the nature of inspiration, see pages 6, 24, and 109.

Why is the Bible so long?

Actually, it isn't—at least not when you compare it to the Scriptures of the Eastern religions, which have many thousands of pages, or when you remember that it is more of a library than a single book. The Bible, at about 1000 pages, is a rich and involved story, and not one that can be told quickly. Novels sometimes reach lengths of 1000 pages, but the biblical story is a true account and infinitely more valuable. Take a few pages a day, and you can easily read it through in a matter of months. If you read it with understanding, it will change your life.

When were the chapter and verse numbers added?

The chapter numbers were not added (or standardized) till the late Middle Ages, and the verse numbers were added in the mid-sixteenth century. Though they are useful for reference, they are not inspired.

When I began reading the Bible, I was taken aback by how short many chapters are—often just a paragraph or two. Yet chapter numbers simply provide a way to find passages. For an example, James 1:27 means the first chapter of James, verse 27. The system takes a little getting used to, though in the end it will help you more efficiently navigate the 1189 chapters and approximately 31,000 verses of the Bible. Rather than read the Bible verse by verse or chapter by chapter, the most efficient way to grow in our comprehension of Scripture is to read book by book.

What language was the Bible originally written in?

Think of the Bible as a library, not a single document. Its books were written and edited over a period of many centuries and originate from many countries. It was written in three languages.

- Ninety-nine percent of the Old Testament was written in Hebrew. Most of the Bible is the Old Testament, so Hebrew is the principal language of Scripture.

- One percent of the Old Testament—271 verses out of about 23,000—was written in Aramaic (Genesis 31:47;

Jeremiah 10:11; Ezra 4:6–6:18; 7:12-26; Daniel 2:4–7:2). Aramaic is closely related to Hebrew and uses the same writing system. A few Aramaic words and phrases appear in the New Testament because the first-century Jews of Palestine (including Jesus) spoke Aramaic.

- The entire New Testament was written in Greek.

None of the Bible was written in Latin, though a Latin translation became standard among the Western church in the early Middle Ages.

Hebrew, Aramaic, and Greek are well understood by scholars, and as a result we can be confident that we are reading accurate versions of the original biblical documents. We should be profoundly grateful for those who've done the laborious work of Bible translation, including past generations of missionaries, linguistic pioneers, and copyists. (But perhaps we should be a little suspicious of preachers who habitually refer to the Greek or Hebrew without continuing to study these languages. If you can't stand the heat, stay out of the kitchen.)

What's the difference between a translation and an interpretation?

A translation takes us from the original language to another, such as from Hebrew to Egyptian (Genesis 42:23) or from Persian to Hebrew (Esther 8:9). An interpretation, on the other hand, is our understanding of the text once we have read it in a language we know. (What does it mean? How do we apply it to our lives?) Of course, translation involves some degree of interpretation. (For example, in going from Spanish to English, the translator must decide whether *señor* means "mister," "sir," or "Lord." Usually the context resolves any ambiguity.)

Doesn't the Bible interpret itself? Doesn't individual interpretation cause dissensions?

Second Peter 1:20 reminds us that the prophets did not play fast and loose with the word of God. When we read Scripture, we're not reading the prophets' opinions. Rather, the word of God is mediated through them. Nonetheless, *interpretation* is not a dirty word. To believe that the Bible interprets itself and that we can understand it without doing any work at all is simply to justify laziness. This is wrong and will lead to simplistic and misguided answers.

Bible study is more than simply reading and obeying. The middle step of interpretation is essential. Some may say, "Don't interpret the Bible; just obey it." This may sound pious, but it is misleading. The *basic* truths of the Bible may be plain for all to see, yet we can understand most of the Scripture only through disciplined study. Interpretation involves comprehending the meaning of a passage in its original context. The Bible never claims that every part is easy to understand (in fact, quite the opposite—2 Peter 3:14-16). It urges us to meditate diligently on God's word (Joshua 1:8; Psalm 119), applying ourselves in hope that the Lord will give insight (2 Timothy 2:7,15).

Surely copyists make some mistakes, so how can the Bible be trustworthy?

Yes, copyists occasionally committed minor errors. An illustration will help. Jesus found the demon-possessed man (Mark 5:1) in the region of the Gerasenes—or was it the Gadarenes? Or the Gergasenes? Geographical confusion on the part of an ancient scribe would be understandable. (Similarly, people today might confuse Newark and New York, or New York City and New York State.) Scholars are not sure which reading is original. But does it matter? Nothing essential is lost through a slight geographical shift.

No surviving manuscript is an exact copy of the original New Testament and Old Testament writings, although many ancient manuscripts are extremely close. The alternative readings listed in the footnotes of your Bible are not contradictions. They are simply instances in which translators were unsure.

Inspiration applies to the original text, not to copies. Most Bible believers do not believe the modern translations are perfect; only the original *autographs* (as scholars call them) are pristine. However, most differences are so minor that to list them would be tiresome. No Christian doctrine is affected.

Do modern translators ever get it wrong?

No modern translation of the Hebrew and Greek text is perfect, though some versions are more accurate than others. The New International Version interprets Psalm 100:3, "It is he who made us, and we are his." Earlier English versions read, "It is he who made us, and not we ourselves." In the older translations, the Hebrew word *lo* (his) was mistaken for the word *lo'* (not) because of a widespread spelling variant. Here's another example: The word translated *disciples* in Acts 11:26 is unfairly softened to *believers* in the paraphrased Living Bible. The original text contains no contradiction.

Variants are bound to occur because Hebrew, the principal language of the Bible, is not as precise as such modern languages as English, Russian, or German. And even New Testament Greek, though more precise than Hebrew, often permits more than one way to translate a word or phrase. People who are unfamiliar with these ancient languages may find what they erroneously assume to be a discrepancy when they compare one modern version to another.

Here are some abbreviations of popular translations:

NIV—New International Version
NASB—New American Standard Bible
KJV—King James Version
NKJV—New King James Version
ESV—English Standard Version
NET—New English Translation
HCSB—Holman Christian Standard Bible
RSV—Revised Standard Version
NRSV—New Revised Standard Version

When translators note, "The meaning of the Hebrew for this word is uncertain," how can we clearly understand the passage in English?

First, let's commend the translators for honestly admitting uncertainty. Translation from one language into another is not an exact science because a single word in the original language may have a range of meanings and may be accurately expressed in many ways in the translation language. Fortunately, relatively few words in the Bible have meanings that elude us, though there are a handful.

Consider Job 21:24: "...his body well nourished, his bones rich with marrow." The sense of the verse is clear enough: The person is physically healthy. But the meaning of the Hebrew word translated *body* is uncertain, and it appears only once in the Old Testament, so we have no other instances to compare. Here is how some other translations read:

- "His sides are filled out with fat, and the marrow of his bones is moist" (NASB).

- "His breasts [or milk pails] are full of milk, and his bones are moistened with marrow" (KJV).

- "His body full of fat and the marrow of his bones moist" (RSV).

- "His entrails are full of fat and the bones of this one are moistened with marrow" (Latin Vulgate).

All translations yield the same general sense. Confusion centers around only one word, the Hebrew *'atin* (milk pail or bucket). We are dealing with figurative language. (Nearly the entire book of Job is poetry, as the NIV indentations and stanzas indicate.) The NIV clearly follows the RSV, avoiding the wooden translation of the medieval Latin. The NASB similarly uses a broad word—*sides*. The Latin *viscera* conveys the same sense as the NASB, while the KJV humorously over-interprets, leading to a biological implausibility.

But regardless of which translation is right, no doctrine of Scripture depends on it, nor is the gist of the passage substantially affected. This is typical of verses that contain obscure words. And though I read every footnote, nothing is wrong with skipping them entirely. Little will be missed.

Why doesn't my Bible have the Apocrypha? And what is the Septuagint, or LXX?

Tradition holds that 70 Jews translated the Old Testament into Greek a couple of centuries before Christ. (*LXX* is Roman for 70, and the Latin word for 70 is *septuaginta*.) This translation included the Apocrypha—a collection of works that were written during the 400-year gap between the Old Testament and New Testament. Some of these apocryphal works contain valuable historical information, but others are of little value as sources. The theology is sometimes inferior, including such doctrines as penance, purgatory, almsgiving for forgiveness, sex for procreation only, prayers to and for the dead, and a host of other objectionable notions.

By the time of the Counter-Reformation, the Apocrypha had been familiar to believers for 1500 years or more and had been included in Bibles for more than a millennium, though it hadn't always been considered to be fully scriptural. (Thus Protestants err if they claim the Apocrypha was added to the Bible in the sixteenth century.) In April 1546, the Roman Church declared these books to be inspired and imposed severe penalties for regarding them as less than authoritative. Moreover, the Orthodox churches have always had these books in their Bible. At the end of the day, little rides on whether or not they are included in the canon; Christians have differing opinions, but the core message of the Bible and the gospel remains unaffected either way.

I disagree b/cause some people believe it. Purgatory etc.

Is the King James Version the only accurate English version?

No. At the turn of the seventeenth century, the translators' understanding of Hebrew grammar was satisfactory but not great. You may recall that their translation enterprise (1605–1611) was three centuries before the Dead Sea Scrolls were discovered (1947) and two and a half centuries before the great papyrus finds in Egypt in the late 1800s that shed so much light on New Testament Greek. (Before this time, some scholars and churchmen supposed that Koine Greek was a divine language because no examples had been found outside of Scripture. As it turns out, this was the everyday language of the home, street, and marketplace!)

The second edition of the KJV corrected some 500 errors. A number of problems still remain, such as the 11 references to unicorns and satyrs. man-goat

In addition to the much-improved understanding of Greek and Hebrew since the seventeenth century, the textual basis of modern English translations has considerably broadened. Many of the manuscripts the KJV translators consulted were only a century or two old. Now we have complete New Testament manuscripts from the fourth century, and the Old Testament manuscripts of the Dead Sea Scrolls are more than a thousand years older than those available in the early 1600s.

The original KJV included the entire Apocrypha. So when people say, "If it was good enough for Jesus and the apostles, it's good enough for me," I wonder if they mean the original KJV, with the Apocrypha, or a later version. Few KJV advocates are willing to accept the inspiration of the apocryphal books.

I also wonder if they understand the meaning of Elizabethan words, such as *conversation.* In 1611, it meant "lifestyle." Today's reader of the KJV will predictably interpret *conversation* as "talk." Languages evolve; they move on. Fresh translations must continually be made. Otherwise the old ones, less and less understood by contemporary readers, will become obstacles to understanding. More than 120 English translations are available today, many of them recently translated and easy to read.

Why do so many numbers in the Bible end in zero? Were people just guessing?

The Bible often uses round numbers and other approximations, especially where large quantities are involved. In Matthew 14 we read of the feeding of the 5000. The passage itself informs us that this is a round number. Further, biblical counting and censuses include only adult males. Acts 2:41 and 4:4 not only record only the male church members but also round the number to the nearest thousand. Further, many numbers in Scripture are symbolic, including 7, 40, and 1000.

In addition, numbers were difficult to copy in ancient manuscripts. They were represented by letters of the alphabet, and they weren't easy to read. (The Hindu-Arabic numbering system that most of us use today evolved slowly and was adopted many centuries after the last New Testament book was written.) For example, 42,360 in Ezra 2:64 is *tessares myriades dischilioi triakosioi hexekonta* in the Greek Septuagint. Such unwieldy expressions meant greater chances of copyist errors, which did occur in some manuscripts. But despite occasional manuscript discrepancies, no biblical doctrine is controverted.

Do God and the Bible view men and women as equals?

Sometimes the New Testament uses the Greek word *adelphe* (sister). More often, it uses *adelphos* (brother or either brother or sister). *Adelphoi* means brothers or siblings, and *adelphai* means sisters (females only). When the writer must choose a pronoun, according to standard practice then (and now), the masculine pronoun is normally used. This does not reflect a sexist bias; it is just a convention.

The Bible strongly upholds the honored place of women. Consider the Ten Commandments. The fifth commandment is conspicuous: "Honor your father and your mother." In the ancient world, mention of the father would not normally be accompanied by a reference to the mother. But there it is, in the Law of Moses, well over a millennium before the time of Christ. Both Testaments include many similar examples.

As we read the Scriptures, we find perspective and encouragement and react less to perceived inequities.

Why does the Bible have two Testaments?

The biblical story unfolds in an amazing plan of fulfillment as God's promises to the patriarchs are inherited by the people of Israel and then by the church of Christ. The Law showed us God's love, wisdom, power, justice, and mercy. Yet it could not deliver us from our sins. Only the new covenant could do that. Note that the Greek *diatheke* means both "testament" and "covenant." The writer to the Hebrews pursues the important connection between a covenant and a testament. See, for example, Hebrews 8:6-13 and 9:15-17.

The Old and New Testaments contain old and new covenants, and these have major differences. Under the Torah (the first five books of the Bible, which record the old covenant or Law), the people of God sacrificed animals. Not so under the new covenant; Jesus himself is the Lamb of God (Leviticus 1; John 1:29; 1 Corinthians 5:7). The change itself was predicted in Jeremiah 31:31-34 and other passages. The Law tolerated polygamy (but never commended it), made more allowance for divorce and war, included oaths, and of course made Sabbath days and years central. Under the new covenant, much has changed. Matthew 5:21-48 stresses this in striking terms. This update, or covenantal modification, is not a contradiction.

Just as we see a transition from the old to the new covenant, numerous biblical doctrines that appear embryonically in the Hebrew Scriptures are well developed by the time of the Greek New Testament. The doctrine of Satan was partially worked out in the Old Testament but completed in the New. The person and role of the Messiah become clearer in the later books of the Old Testament and are revealed and explained in the New. God's presence progresses from the Garden of Eden to the tabernacle to the temple to the church to the heavenly city, which is symbolically depicted in Revelation. These are examples of progressive revelation.

Consider this analogy. My first-grade teacher never told us about long division; the concept is beyond most six-year-olds. And my algebra teacher did not explain trigonometry. Was this deception? Of course not. Each stage progressively builds on the previous level. I eventually took three years of calculus, but even then I realized that my professors knew more than they told. A good teacher does not get too far ahead of the students (Mark 4:33). In the same way, God revealed his will in the pages of Scripture gradually.

Are we to read the Bible literally or figuratively?

The answer is yes. Read literally when dealing with straightforward language, figuratively otherwise. Is it really "raining cats and dogs" when heavy precipitation falls to the earth? Of course not; we understand what figures of speech really mean. In the same vein, are we to literally believe in rivers clapping their hands, stones crying out, or stars plummeting to the earth (Psalm 98:8; Luke 19:40; Revelation 6:13)? We need to distinguish the medium from the message. Sometimes the medium is colorful and poetic; at other times it is prosaic. And sometimes a biblical writer picks up a familiar theme or reshapes a preexisting piece of literature to tell the truth about God. A few examples are the parable of the rich man and Lazarus, the flood narrative, and the destruction of the primeval monster Rahab, all of which circulated in one form or another in the ancient world (Luke 16:19-31; Genesis 6:9-9:17; Psalm 89:10).

Once we discern the type of literature we are reading—and usually this is not too difficult—we can take the passage at face value. That is the best way to fully appreciate the inspired word of God.

If we should read every passage in the Bible literally...

- Even Australian Aborigines bought grain from Joseph during the famine (Genesis 41:57).
- The crocodile (leviathan) breathes fire (Job 41:20).

- God has feathers (Psalm 91:4).

- Solomon's bride had birds in her head (Song of Solomon 4:1).

- Edom is still on fire, and the smoke is visible in the Middle East today (Isaiah 34:9-10).

- There will be more widows in Judah than humans on the planet (Jeremiah 15:8).

- We can make the Matterhorn jump into the Mediterranean (Mark 11:23).

- Anna *never* left the temple. Never (Luke 2:37).

- Paul died more than 12,000 times between his baptism and beheading (1 Corinthians 15:31).

- Dogs performed circumcisions in the first century (Philippians 3:2).

- Godless men are made of salt water (Jude 13).

- Jesus is made of wood. Or is it burning hydrogen? (Revelation 22:16).

What's the best way to learn biblical Hebrew and Greek?

The best advice I can give is to study the biblical languages in a university language class. To master any language—especially an ancient one—requires structure and accountability (including classes, assignments, quizzes, and exams). You can buy do-it-yourself books, and these may provide a helpful introduction as long as they are followed by college-level instruction. Otherwise, "half-learning" is the best you will do—which is worse than knowing nothing. Alexander Pope said, "A little learning is a dang'rous thing / Drink deep, or touch not the Pierian spring."

Is today's Bible complete?

The subject of canonization (how the Bible came together) is probably the most complex subject in all of Christian history. Here is a brief introduction.

- Jesus himself affirmed the inspiration of the Old Testament Scriptures (Luke 24:25-27,44).

- The old covenant anticipates the new, particularly in such books as Isaiah (59:19-21), Jeremiah (31:31-34), and Ezekiel (36:24-27).

- The inspiration of the New Testament is also guaranteed by its apostolic connection to Jesus Christ (John 14:26; 16:12-13; Galatians 1:11-12; 2 Peter 1:12-18). Jesus explained that the Spirit would enable his followers to relay the gospel message and its implications.

- The New Testament expresses confident assurance that the Old Testament is inspired (Romans 15:4; 1 Corinthians 10:11; 2 Timothy 3:14-17) and that it is fulfilled in the ministry of Jesus Christ (Matthew 5:17-20; Acts 1:16; 3:18).

- Jews and Christians produced far more writings than the few that were considered canonically inspired. But the Jewish works were penned later than the close of the Old Testament canon, and the Christian ones came generations after the apostolic period.

The message of the Bible is presented multiple times and in various ways. Even if a few books of the Bible were removed or further words of the prophets or apostles were discovered, no substantive revision to the faith would likely be necessary.

Fear that something might be missing is similar to a fear that the *Mona Lisa* would be forever lost if a couple of brush strokes were undone or an extra one added. This would likely make little difference, if any. Everyone knows the original was not bearded or horned. And so, through the ages she smiles at her admirers.

Do any Bible passages tell us to read the Bible every day?

Daily study is a healthy spiritual discipline, but we must not legislate when the Lord has not spoken.

One passage intimates the blessing of daily study (Proverbs 8:34), and another mandates it for the king (Deuteronomy 17:18-20), though not for every Israelite. And God commanded Joshua to meditate on the law day and night (Joshua 1:8). We also have the wholesome example of the Bereans (Acts 17:11), who were examining the Scriptures every day to see if Paul's message was true. But no Scripture explicitly requires daily Bible study. Of course, we are to delight in and meditate on the word of God (Psalm 119).

In our day, when Bibles are relatively inexpensive, why wouldn't anyone want to read daily? It is such a privilege. I know of no better way to study and appreciate the Scriptures. The lack of zeal for the Scriptures prevalent among so many wearing the name of Christ is truly shocking. We need to be sobered by the biblical illiteracy of our generation—and I refer not only to those outside the community of Christ. Verses like Hosea 4:6, Hosea 8:12, Jeremiah 8:7, and Jeremiah 15:16 challenge us to the quick. Knowing the word of the Lord is essential to knowing the Lord himself (1 Samuel 3:7).

Although the Bible does not require daily study, it is a life-giving habit, a good one to commit to for the rest of your life.

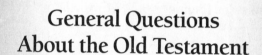

2

General Questions
About the Old Testament

What is a testament?

A testament is a document that defines a covenant and that one has sworn to be true. The Old Testament records the covenant between God and Israel (enacted in Exodus) as well as the related 39 books of law, prophecy, and other Jewish writings.

When was the Old Testament written?

The books of the Old Testament were written at many different times, so there is no single year of publication—as in "Almighty, the Lord, *The Old Testament* (Jerusalem: Word of God Press, 400 BC)." In fact, its 39 books clearly point to 70 or 80 original sources, some dating as far back as the second millennium BC.

How old is the oldest surviving Old Testament copy?

The oldest copy of *all* the Old Testament books in Hebrew dates from the ninth century AD. However, the crucial discovery of the Dead Sea Scrolls brought to light thousands of fragments from the century or two before Christ—that is, a millennium older than the medieval manuscripts. And the degree of textual correspondence is impressive. In addition, the Jews translated the Hebrew into Greek (around 250 BC), and manuscript fragments survive from the second century BC. We have relatively complete Greek Old Testaments from the fourth century AD. Finally, the oldest Old Testament manuscript of which I am aware (Numbers 6:24-26), discovered in 1977, dates to the sixth century BC.

Who are the main characters in the Old Testament?

The three principal human characters are Abraham, the father of the faithful; Moses, the giver of the Law; and David, the great king and sweet psalmist of Israel. They lived approximately 4000, 3300, and 3000 years ago, respectively. Of course the central character of the Bible is God.

What is Israel?

Israel is a person, a nation, and a place. As a personal name, it is the epithet of Jacob, the grandson of Abraham. Jacob had 12 sons, each of whom gave rise to a tribe (except for Joseph, whose sons Ephraim and Manasseh each became a tribe). These tribes grew while in slavery in Egypt, and after the exodus, they became the nation of Israel (Exodus 19:6). As a place, *Israel* has several meanings. The land of Israel is located in Southwest Asia, east of Africa and southwest of Europe. Unfortunately, due to poor leadership, the kingdom split during the reign of Solomon's son Rehoboam (931 BC). The new northern kingdom retained the name Israel, and the southern kingdom was called Judah.

What is a Gentile?

In the Bible, a Gentile is simply a non-Jew. To convert, a Gentile had to be circumcised and follow the Law of Moses, especially the

Sabbath and kosher laws. In New Testament times, Gentiles hesitating to undergo the minor surgery entailed in conversion were described as "God fearing" (Acts 10:2,22; 13:26,50; 17:4,17). Women could become Jews too—obviously, more easily than men. Confessing faith in the God of Israel, offering a sacrifice at the temple, and undergoing ritual washing were normal. In rabbinic times, proselyte baptism was added. From the Jewish perspective, there are only two categories of persons: Jews and Gentiles.

What is the meaning of *Middle East*? East of what?

From the perspective of the Old World (that is, Europe before the colonization of the Americas, or New World), the East stretched roughly from Turkey to Japan. In the parlance of the nineteenth century, the Near East consisted of the Balkan states of southeastern Europe and the western part of the continent of Asia. The Far East included the countries bordering the Pacific Ocean and its associated seas, and the Middle East included such countries as Afghanistan and Pakistan.

Today the term *Near East* is rare, though one occasionally finds it used synonymously with *Middle East*. Rather, the term *Middle East* is the common designation for the predominantly Muslim nations of Southwest Asia, such as Saudi Arabia, Iraq, and Syria.

What was the difference between the tabernacle and the temple?

The tabernacle, following the blueprints in Exodus, was a portable temple, constructed while Moses led the people of Israel in the desert. Several centuries after Moses' death, once Israel was established in the promised land, Solomon built a permanent temple. The tabernacle was made of wood and animal skins, but the temple was built of wood and stone.

What is the promised land?

The promised land, or Canaan, was the territory between the

Mediterranean Sea and the Jordan River, with Egypt to the south and west and Lebanon to the north. The 12 tribes also secured territory east of the Jordan River. The promised land was somewhat larger than the present state of Israel.

The promised land was described as a land flowing with milk and honey (Exodus 3:8). As those who live in the Middle East know, the first element refers to goats' milk. The second is thought to refer to honey from dates, though in 2007 a large apiary was discovered, so now the possibility of honey from bees must also be considered.

Did the Jews write anything after the Old Testament and before Jesus was born?

Yes, quite a lot. The apocryphal literature (Wisdom of Solomon, Sirach, Tobit, Judith, 1–2 Maccabees, 1–2 Esdras, Baruch, and additions to Daniel, Esther, and Jeremiah) was penned between 400 and 50 BC. Interestingly, by the time the Christian church was taking a serious interest in the Apocrypha, the Jews were losing interest. It remains part of the Old Testament in the Catholic and Orthodox church, though considered "deuterocanonical" (of second order canonicity). It has much to offer, filling in the intertestamental picture historically and theologically.

Why is God so much nicer in the New Testament than in the Old?

God in the Old Testament is a God of judgment, grace, wisdom, and love. For a list of his attributes, read his "name" in Exodus 34:5-7. The Old Testament includes far more verses on the love of God than does the New Testament. And while both Testaments present a message of judgment, we read of hell in the New Testament—particularly in Jesus' own teaching. It will not do to have two separate Gods—one of high expectations, one of low; one on a short fuse, the other patient and forgiving. Whatever is true of God in the Old Testament is also true of him in the New Testament, and his sometimes seemingly opposite attributes must be seen in perspective and balance (Romans 11:22).

Still, the Old Testament is marked by warfare, the flood, the Canaanite genocide, capital punishments, deportations, and exiles, all of which stand in stark contrast to the ministry of Jesus Christ, the Prince of Peace. The old covenant was more physical than the new. Rewards for obedience included good health, agricultural prosperity, wealth, and long life. Punishments for disobedience included sickness, famine, and military defeat (Leviticus 26; Deuteronomy 28). The new covenant does not rule out all temporal blessings, but the primary blessings are spiritual. In contrast to ancient Israel, the church is not a political entity.

The New Testament proclaims that the God of the Old Testament, the one who created us for fellowship with himself, has appeared in the person of Jesus Christ. "I the LORD do not change" (Malachi 3:6). Astonishingly, the New Testament equates the Lord of the Old Testament with the Lord Jesus Christ.

Why do most people read the New Testament more than the Old Testament?

More than 75 percent of the Bible is the Old Testament. The New Testament is better known among Christians because it more explicitly teaches about Christ. Yet since the Old Testament is the foundation for the New Testament, those who ignore it do so to their own detriment. A true Bible believer will study the entire Bible, and a church devoted to the Bible does not preach only from the New Testament.

As I travel around the world, I am continually amazed how few believers have ever read the Old Testament. My estimate is that no more than 10 percent of Christians have completed the Old Testament. If you have never read the whole Old Testament, why not set a goal to complete it sometime in the next year?

Book Names
in the Old Testament

Genesis to Deuteronomy

- *Genesis*—The Greek word for origin. The book lays out the origins of the cosmos, mankind, and the major human institutions.

- *Exodus*—Latin, from the Greek *exodos* (exit). Records Israel's exit from Egyptian slavery.

- *Leviticus*—Latin for "pertaining to Levi," one of the 12 sons of Jacob. His descendants were responsible for worship and sacrifice, which are important topics of this book.

- *Numbers*—Includes two censuses, or numberings, of the people of Israel.

- *Deuteronomy*—From the Greek word *deuteronomion* (second law). Restates the law shortly before the Israelites enter Canaan.

Joshua to 2 Kings

- *Joshua*—Named after Moses' successor, the military commander who led God's people into the promised land. In Hebrew, *Joshua* means "savior." The names *Joshua* and *Jesus* are identical in Hebrew as well as in Greek.

- *Judges*—Named after the leaders, or judges, of God's people before Israel's first king (approximately 1400–1050 BC). The judges led only a handful of tribes at a time, and their periods of leadership overlap somewhat.

- *Ruth*—Named after its heroine, Ruth (Hebrew for companion or friend), this book describes life in the period of the judges.

- *1 and 2 Samuel*—Named after Israel's first judge. *Samuel* means "God has heard." Samuel is a major character through much of 1 Samuel but not 2 Samuel.

- *1 and 2 Kings*—Describes life in Israel under the monarchy.

During most of this period, Israel was divided in two: Israel in the north and Judah in the south were perennially at odds with one another.

(In the Hebrew Bible, the books from Joshua to 2 Kings were known as "the former prophets.")

1 Chronicles to Esther

All of these are *exilic* books. That is, they were written after the Babylonians had broken down the wall around Jerusalem, destroyed the temple and many of the buildings, and taken the people of Judah (the southern kingdom of the original nation of Israel) into captivity.

- *1* and *2 Chronicles*—Chronicle the reigns of the kings, particularly those of Judah. These were the last of the Old Testament books to be written and date from the fifth century BC.

- *Ezra* and *Nehemiah*—Perhaps originally one book, these are named after two of the key figures in the rebuilding of Israel after the exile. *Ezra* is similar to the Hebrew word for *help*, and *Nehemiah* sounds like "God is my comfort."

- *Esther*—Named for the heroine of the book, a Jewess who landed in the harem of King Xerxes. *Esther* means "star" and is the name of a popular goddess throughout much of Old Testament history. This woman is anything but an idolater, however. Through her courage and her royal position, she saves the people of God from a Persian holocaust.

Job to Song of Solomon

- *Job*—Named after the man whose world (and theology) is thrown into confusion as he personally confronts the problem of suffering.

- *Psalms*—Originally prayers and hymns sung to the accompaniment of stringed instruments. (*Psallo* is old Greek for "pluck.")

- *Proverbs*—A collection of hundreds of wise sayings from Solomon and other contributors.

- *Ecclesiastes*—From the Latin word for the leader of the assembly *(ecclesia)*, presumably referring to Solomon, the traditional author.

- *Song of Solomon*—A romantic poem or collection of poems for the marriage of Solomon. Also called Song of Songs and Canticles.

Isaiah to Daniel

These final 16 books are attributed to the prophets.

- *Isaiah*—This great prophet of the eighth century BC is the most frequently quoted prophet in the New Testament. His name means "Yahweh is salvation."

- *Jeremiah*—This prophet of Judah ministered during Jerusalem's fall (626–586 BC). The meaning of his name is uncertain.

- *Lamentations*—Jeremiah's laments over the destruction of Jerusalem, the temple, and the kingdom of Judah. To make matters worse, the prophets, priests, and kings would not listen to Jeremiah.

- *Ezekiel*—While Jeremiah stayed in Jerusalem, Ezekiel prophesied among the exiles in Babylon (sixth century BC). His name means "God is strong" or "God makes strong."

- *Daniel*—A statesman and prophet who had been deported to Babylon in the late 600s BC. One of the Bible's outstanding examples of faithfulness. His name appropriately means "God is my judge."

Hosea to Malachi

- *Hosea, Joel,* and *Amos*—Prophets in the eighth century BC. Their names mean, respectively, "He (Yahweh) has helped," "Yahweh is God," and "burdensome" or "burdenbearer."

- *Obadiah*—A sixth-century BC prophet who challenged Edom not to gloat over Jerusalem's fall. The name means "servant of Yahweh."

- *Jonah*—A prophet in the eighth century BC. Ironically, *Jonah* means "dove"—despite the prophet's prejudicial attitude and behavior in Jonah 4.

- *Micah*—Means "Who is like Yahweh (God)?" Dates from the eighth century BC.

- *Nahum*—Means "comfort." Nahum prophesied against Assyria in the seventh century BC.

- *Habakkuk* and *Zephaniah*—Prophets in the seventh century BC. Their names mean "embrace" and "Yahweh has treasured."

- *Haggai* and *Zechariah*—Prophets in the sixth century BC. Their names mean "festal" and "Yahweh remembers," respectively.

- *Malachi*—Possibly named after a prophet in the fifth century BC. *Malachi* means "my angel" or "my messenger" (see Malachi 3:1).

3

General Questions About the New Testament

What does the name *Jesus Christ* actually mean?

Jesus means "salvation." In both Hebrew (*Yeshua*) and Greek (*Yesous*), this same word is also translated *Joshua*.

Christ is from the Greek *Christos* (anointed one). The first Greek letter of this word is *chi*, written *X* (as in *Xmas*). Of course *Christ* is a title, not a last name.

What's the difference between *Messiah* and *Christ*?

There is no difference. *Christ* (Greek: *Christos*) and *Messiah* (Hebrew: *Mashiach*) both mean "anointed one." In the Old Testament, prophets, priests, and kings were anointed. In Jesus, the three streams converge. He is the ultimate prophet, a great high priest, and the King of kings. He is the central character in the biblical story. As others have said, history is his story.

When was the New Testament written?

The New Testament was produced from the late 40s to the mid-90s AD. The earliest document was probably Galatians (AD 48), though James may have been written in the same decade. The Gospels were probably penned in this order: Mark, Matthew, Luke, John. Scholars believe the latest parts of the New Testament are the works of John (1, 2, and 3 John, Revelation, and the Gospel of John, although some scholars place the Gospel four or five decades earlier). Thus the entire New Testament was written during the span of half a century.

Why are there four Gospels?

All four accounts of the words and life of Jesus were written within a few decades of his lifetime, and the early church recognized all four as inspired and apostolic documents. Each targets a particular audience and contains unique data and emphases, affording us a stereoscopic and textured view of Jesus Christ.

Who are the main characters in the New Testament?

Besides Jesus, the most influential and prolific individuals are the apostles Peter, John, and Paul. Luke wrote more words in the New Testament than any other author, but he remains behind the scenes. As is the case with the Old Testament, the complete cast of characters is large.

How can we differentiate between characters in the Bible who share the same name, like James the brother of Jesus and James the brother of John?

Commentaries or chain references will nearly always clear up any confusion about who's who. James is a good case in point because at least four men in the New Testament share this name. The more colorful are James the Just (the brother of Jesus), who was stoned to death (as recorded by the first-century Jewish historian Josephus), and James the son of Zebedee, who was beheaded by the Romans (Acts 12:1-2).

When was Jesus born? When was he crucified?

Seven hundred years before Jesus was born, Isaiah prophesied his birth, life, and sacrificial death in great detail (Isaiah 7; 9; 11; 42; 53; 61). Copies of Isaiah have survived from 100 BC and are on display in the Israel Museum in Jerusalem. Yet the prophecies never specified the exact year. Christ was most likely born in Bethlehem between 7 and 5 BC. (Herod the Great, who tried to kill him, died in 4 BC.) This fulfilled the ancient prophecy of Micah 5:2. Our calendar, which was created by Julius Caesar in 45 BC, with slight modification in 1582, has Jesus being born after his true birthday.

As for his death, Jesus was crucified in May of the year AD 30, when he was in his midthirties. Crucifixion was not a penalty inflicted on Roman citizens except in cases of treason. It was reserved for slaves and revolutionaries.

What language did Jesus and the apostles speak?

Jesus was probably trilingual. In Galilee (the northern part of Israel, where Jesus was raised), the native tongue was Aramaic—a language still spoken today in some quarters. The New Testament includes some Aramaic words, such as *Maranatha, Golgotha, Gethsemane, Gabbatha, Hakeldama, Hosanna,* and *ephphatha.* Aramaic was not the only tongue heard in first-century Palestine; so was Greek. Scholars of the Torah also spoke Hebrew.

Why are Jesus' words printed in red in some editions of the Bible?

Editions of the New Testament with Jesus' words in red, first appearing in 1899, were intended as an aid to teach the world about Christ and the gospel. The implication, in the minds of many, was that the words of Christ are more inspired than the words in black, as though the writings of John, Paul, and others deserve less study. Yet while Jesus Christ is supreme, the Spirit works through *all* Scripture (John 14:26; 2 Timothy 3:16; 2 Peter 3:16). To separate out the words of Christ is to create a false dichotomy.

What is the gospel?

Gospel (in this book, with a lowercase *g*) is an older English word meaning "good news." Also called the *evangel*, it's the story of God's initiative and his desire to forgive and have a relationship with us based on the historic events of Christ's death, burial, and resurrection (1 Corinthians 15:1-5). It means that there is hope for our lives—the opportunity to know the Lord and live life as he intended. The gospel message requires a response (2 Thessalonians 1:8).

Gospel (with a capital *G*) is also the literary genre of the first four books of the New Testament, which record Jesus' teachings and the events of his life—the gospel story.

Christ died to set us free from the law. Do Christians still have to obey the Bible?

We aren't made right with God by following the Law of Moses. Jesus brings freedom from empty, dead religion. Yet the New Testament does not lower the standard of commitment. If anything, Jesus has raised the bar (Matthew 5:17-48). The New Testament frequently stresses obedience to God's commands (Matthew 7:21-23, 28:19-20; John 14:15-24; Acts 5:32; 2 Thessalonians 1:8; 1 John 2:3-6, 5:3; Revelation 14:12).

Did Jesus' death prove he was a failure?

On the cross, God's justice, mercy, and wisdom meet our desperate human need for forgiveness and hope. We deserve to answer for our sins; Jesus willingly takes our place. Greatness is manifested in humility, and true greatness is serving others, not having others serve you (Mark 10:43-45; Philippians 2:5-11). The way up is the way down. The deep paradox of the cross is not only the plan of God but also our motivation for living a *cruciform* life. Embracing the will of God, we are impelled to say no to self and yes to him. For more, see the question and answer on Luke 9:23.

Book Names
of the New Testament

- *Matthew* to *John*—Gospels named after their traditional authors.

- *Acts of the Apostles*—Would have been better named Acts of Peter and Paul or Acts of the Holy Spirit. Written by Luke.

- *Romans* to *2 Thessalonians*—Paul's letters to churches, arranged longest to shortest.

- *1 Timothy* to *Philemon*—Paul's letters to individuals, arranged longest to shortest.

- *Hebrews*—Apparently written to Jewish Christians. The author is unknown.

- *James*—*Iacobos* in Greek and *Ya'akov* in Hebrew, also translated *Jacob* in English. This James was a brother of Jesus Christ, not the brother of John.

- *1 Peter* to *Jude*—Letters written by the apostles Peter and John, and by Jude, a brother of Jesus Christ.

- *Revelation*—*Apocalypsis* (unveiling) in Greek. In this book the veil is pulled back, and we take an inspired peek behind the scenes at true spiritual reality. The alternate English title is the Apocalypse.

QUESTIONS ABOUT OLD TESTAMENT BOOKS

4

Genesis

Genesis 1:1—When was the earth created? Does the Bible tell us how old the universe is?

Genesis doesn't include a date for the creation. Some Sunday school curricula say 4004 BC, which was the guess of the Irish Archbishop James Ussher (1581–1656), professor of theological controversies at Trinity College in Dublin. By combining the ages of Genesis 5, he arrived at the dates of 4004 BC for the creation and 2349 BC for the flood. Some 90 percent of American evangelicals believe in a "young earth" (Just a few thousand years old). Yet this approach is not without problems.

We cannot simply add genealogies together (Genesis 4; 5; 10; 11) and arrive at solid dates, because they often skip generations and are based on criteria no longer considered trustworthy. Even if this methodology were sound, dating Genesis 1:1 remains impossible because it precedes the first creation day. As a case in point, we have written records from Egypt and Mesopotamia from before 3000 BC, and the great pyramids of Egypt are some 4500 years old, so Ussher's flood is way too late. Tree-ring dating brings us to millennia before the pyramids, and geological and astronomical study to eons many magnitudes more ancient. Unless the Lord has faked scientific data, the cosmos appears unspeakably older than Ussher's estimate. Since (1) Christians hold a number of views about the age of the world, (2) the Bible is not a science book, and (3) none of these opinions affects the core message of the Scriptures, the best answer is this: The world was created "in the beginning."[1]

Genesis 1:1—Why does the Bible use a plural name (*Elohim*) for the one God?

Elohim is plural in form, but that doesn't mean the Israelites used it with a plural meaning. The city names *Colosse* and *Sardis* are also plural forms, yet they refer to individual cities (Colossians 1:2; Revelation 3:1). Elohim may represent a faint echo of polytheistic times, but this is by no means clear. Many Christians see the Trinity in the plural pronoun, and of course it is possible that the three-in-one God is deliberating in an ongoing dialogue among Father, Son, and Spirit. Yet this is difficult to prove.

Most likely, this is a "plural of majesty," as when the queen of England might say, "We are not amused." Plural though it may be, *Elohim* is used in a singular way. The plurals that follow ("Let us make man…") are simply grammatical necessities.

Genesis 1:1—Is the Big Bang theory compatible with the Bible?

According to a 2010 research of the National Science Foundation, only 33 percent of Americans agree that the universe began with an explosion. Yet nearly all Christian theologians, philosophers, and scientists accept the Big Bang—persons as distinguished as J.P. Moreland, William Lane Craig, Paul Copan, Norman Geisler, Chuck Colson, and John Polkinghorne. Yet for some Bible believers, the Big Bang is anathema. But why? There is much in the Big Bang theory that agrees with the Bible. Formulated in the first half of the twentieth century, it suggests that space and time had a beginning. Though the theory is complex, its simplicity is astounding. Everything we see all began in a single moment in the distant past. Science and theology converge.

Before the theory was proposed—empirical confirmation came only in 1965—most scientists supposed an infinite universe and opposed the Big Bang. Yet the evidence shows the universe had a beginning. So if nothing existed before the beginning, what caused it? A beginning requires a Beginner—God. Whether or not the Big Bang theory ever needs to be revised or updated, there is nothing in it that nullifies faith in God.

Genesis 1:3–2:3—Was the world made in seven literal days?

Through Christian history, perhaps the majority of Christian writers have answered *no* to this question. Such illustrious thinkers from the earliest centuries of the church as Justin Martyr, Clement of Alexandria, Cyprian, and Augustine reckoned the days were not 24-hour periods. In fact, there is more than one way to read the text, and there are at least five major approaches to Genesis 1. It should be emphasized that each interpretation is taught by persons who believe in the Bible and hold the Genesis account to be true. This is one of many areas in which genuine Bible believers do not always see eye to eye. The real question is, which view makes best sense of the facts and the text?

1. The literal theory. God created everything in six literal 24-hour days. As I mentioned, many Christian teachers from AD 100 to 500 did not subscribe to this view. In roughly 2000 pages of commentary on the six creation days, the favored view from the early church is that each day represented a longer period of time, such as a thousand years. This seems to be the simplest view, except that if the account is intended as a literal chronicle of what happened, it is at odds with the scientific evidence.

2. The gap theory. A universal cataclysm took place in a gap between Genesis 1:1 and 1:2. The original creation was destroyed, and

God started over. The dinosaurs were exterminated, their fossils preserved in the ground. Isaiah 45:18 is cited for support: "[The Lord] did not create [the earth] to be empty, but formed it to be inhabited." If the earth was not originally empty, it must have become empty through some global cataclysm, and the six days are God's *re-creation* of the earth. This view is not widely held.

3. *The revelatory day theory.* How did the Genesis writer know what happened at creation? This theory suggests God revealed what happened in stages on seven successive days. This attempt to reconcile Genesis with the apparent antiquity of the earth has few adherents today.

4. *The day-age theory.* Popular among Bible believers, this proposes that each day is a geologic age. Genesis 1 and modern geology have some points of agreement:

- The ancient earth became increasingly ordered.
- The conditions for life preceded the existence of life.
- Simpler forms precede more complex forms.
- Man appears as the highest product of the creative process.

Like the two previous views, this allows for the ancient earth evidenced by science, although there are several discrepancies. Is there another explanation?

5. *The literary theory.* The days are not literal, but are a literary device for communicating the truth about the creation. The original readers of Genesis, sharing the author's culture, understood exactly what he meant. The scheme is logical, not chronological. It also has the marks of poetry. (Other poetic accounts of creation are found in Job 38–41; Psalms 8; 19; 33; 104; 148; Proverbs 8.)

The literary theory recognizes providence. God was preparing the world for habitation. He did this with care, not haste. This theory recognizes a definite structure to the creation account, a schema. Consider how God's providence and forethought are portrayed as each of the first three days prepares for the last three. The world is not an accident, but the result of the wise and caring oversight of the Lord God.

The Creation	
day one: light	day four: light bearers
day two: sky and sea	day five: birds and fish
day three: dry land	day six: land animals and plants
day seven: rest	

Genesis 1 does not purport to be a scientific record of what happened. It is a carefully constructed account, however, based on the use of symbolic numbers, especially three, seven, and ten.

- *Three.* "God said" occurs ten times—three times in reference to man and seven times for all other creatures. There are three blessings. The verb *to create* is used on three occasions and three times on the third occasion.

- *Seven.* "And it was so" occurs seven times, as does "And God saw that it was good." God either names or blesses things seven times. These are all independent of the structure of the seven days. Genesis 1:1 has seven Hebrew words, 1:2 has fourteen words, and 2:1-3 (the seventh paragraph) has thirty-five words—all multiples of seven. The word *earth* occurs twenty-one times, and *Elohim* (God) thirty-five times.

- *Ten.* The names of God occur seventy (seven times ten) times in Genesis 1–4 and prove the unity of the passage. *Yahweh* (God's personal name; see Exodus 6:3) occurs ten times, *Yahweh Elohim* (the Lord God) occurs twenty times, and *Elohim* (God) occurs forty times.

Scholars of the text have discovered a masterful inner structure. Many words and phrases recur a theologically elegant number of times. The chance that this is coincidence is extraordinarily small.

Such observations, as well as the style and poetic aspect of Genesis 1, favor the literary view. Christians who hold to this view, or at least embrace an ancient earth (rejecting literal creation days) include such incisive thinkers as philosopher Francis Schaeffer, apologists Hugh Ross and Norman Geisler, church historian Mark Noll, and writer C.S. Lewis. In fact, at the second summit of the International Council on Biblical Inerrancy in October 1978, the age of the universe was discussed at some length. The conclusion of all the Old Testament scholars and theologians present (such as R.C. Sproul, Norman Geisler, and J.I. Packer) was that inerrancy requires belief in creation but not in 24-hour creation days.

Genesis 1:11,24—Are evolution and the Bible compatible?

As we have seen, the Bible often uses metaphors and word pictures to reveal truth. (See the introduction [page 5], "Are we to read the Bible literally or figuratively?" [page 24], and "How should we read the poetry of the Bible?" [page 109].) When Genesis says that God formed man from the dust, are we reading a technical biological description of the origins of human physiology, or are the Scriptures something else through image and story? In the Genesis account, is the Lord literally a gardener (3:8)? A potter (2:7)? He is the Creator, and these images get that vital point across clearly, even though they need not be read literally. Here are five important points that will help us keep the issue of evolution in perspective.

1. Evolution has nothing whatsoever to do with the existence of God. Evolution is an attempt to account for how life came to be as it is. Whether God used evolution, instantaneous creation, or some other means is irrelevant to the fact of his existence. Evolution concerns the mechanisms of life, not the presence or absence of a Creator.

2. Evolution neither confirms nor disconfirms the Bible. The Scriptures do not commit us to any particular scientific position, so we are free to weigh the evidence and decide for ourselves.

3. *Evolution is not a matter of salvation.* In my first year or two as a Christian, as a young-earth creationist, I was convinced quite to the contrary. It was unthinkable that anyone could disagree (with me) on such an obviously important matter and still remain in the grace of God. But in fact, Christians hold a variety of views on this subject. Even James Orr, whose *The Fundamentals* gave rise to the epithet *fundamentalist* a century ago, described himself as a theistic evolutionist.

4. *There is no conspiracy.* According to the same National Science Foundation study cited above, only 45 percent of Americans agreed with the statement, "Human beings…developed from earlier species of animals." Despite the collective paranoia of those who imagine a massive conspiracy afoot among scientists to reject the Bible, none exists. The majority of scientists believe in a God, and many believe in the Bible.

5. *The biological issues are extremely complex.* The Bible never purports to be a science text. The conviction with which we hold our opinions about science ought to be based on our scientific expertise in the respective area. One does not become a physicist by reading Genesis 1:1-3. In the same way, Genesis 1:11-13 is not the last word on botany. To those who see a scientific account in Genesis 1, we might ask, does Genesis attempt to explain *how* the Lord intended the land to produce vegetation and animal life (1:11,24)? We need to blend humility with courage to embrace truth as we approach matters scientific. Consider Billy Graham's gracious words:

> I believe that God did create the universe. I believe that God created man, and whether it came by an evolutionary process and at a certain point He took this person or being and made him a living soul or not, does not change the fact that God did create man…Whichever way God did it makes no difference as to what man is and man's relationship to God.[2]

C.S. Lewis also had a gracious and sensible approach to this issue:

"I am not either attacking or defending Evolution. I believe that Christianity can still be believed, even if Evolution is true."[3]

Evolution is the official position of the Roman Catholic Church, and the majority of Protestant intellectuals also believe God may have worked through natural processes. Francis Collins, director of the Human Genome Project, is probably the most recognizable American scientist of our time. He is also an evangelical Christian. Other believers who affirm that God created the world through evolutionary processes include such eminent scientists as Oxford's Alister McGrath (PhD in molecular biophysics), Canadian biologist Denis Lamoureux (who holds three doctorates), and Brown University's Kenneth Miller. Even Michael Behe, author of *Darwin's Black Box* and arguably the leading scientist within the Intelligent Design movement, has acknowledged the validity of common descent in his recent book *The Edge of Evolution*.

Founder of Redeemer Presbyterian Church in New York City and *New York Times* bestselling author Timothy Keller correctly notes that creation science was not the traditional response to Darwin; Christians tended to be old-earth creationists.

> I personally take the view that Genesis 1 and 2 relate to each other the way Judges 4 and 5 and Exodus 14 and 15 do…I think Genesis 1 has the earmarks of poetry and is therefore a "song" about the wonder and meaning of God's creation… There will always be debates about how to interpret some passages—including Genesis 1. But it is false logic to argue that if one part of Scripture can't be taken literally then none of it can be.[4]

All of this suggests that like the Big Bang, evolution should not be a problem area for faith. When we are asked to choose between God and evolution, we are being confronted with a false choice. Ultimately, interpretations of biology and Genesis are not matters of salvation, and true Christians differ widely in their views on the origins of life.

Genesis 1:27—Did Adam have a belly button?

Some people teach that God created the earth with an appearance of age, that science is on target in its analysis that the cosmos appears to be billions of years old, but the Bible is right that the earth has been around only a few thousand years. According to the omphalos theory, popularized by Philip Henry Gosse in 1857 and named after the Greek word *omphalos* (navel), Adam was formed as a fully adult male without a mother, so he had no belly button. He may have looked 25 or 30 years old, but in fact he was only seconds old. The trees of Eden, by the same token, would have shown tree rings (annual growth rings). God made the earth with a built-in appearance of age.

But scientific proof cannot be claimed for both a young earth *and* an appearance of age, which is precisely what many young-earth advocates do. You cannot have it both ways. If the omphalos theory is correct, there should be no shred of evidence for a young earth. This approach makes God a party to deceit because he is misleading us through the data of the physical world. Scripture affirms that God reveals truth through the creation (Psalm 19:1-4; Romans 1:20).

When we gaze at the stars, we understand God's wisdom, power, and artistry, and we are moved to worship. Gazing at Adam's navel is another matter.

Genesis 1:28—Is environmentalism irrelevant because the earth is going to burn anyway?

Regrettably, this is the attitude of many religious conservatives, while those who take a lower view of the Bible's inspiration are more likely to rally behind ecological causes. This should not be. The Bible often stresses responsible stewardship (Genesis 1:28) and shows ecological concern even in extreme circumstances (Deuteronomy 20:19). Polluting (on the corporate level), littering (on the individual level), and failing to appreciate the beautiful planet with which we have been entrusted (on the spiritual level) are more than signs that we are not grateful. They are sinful.

Genesis 2:22—Was Eve made from Adam's rib? If so, does this support male chauvinism?

Genesis portrays the Lord as a potter (2:7), a gardener (3:8), and a surgeon (2:21-22). Of course, God could have literally created Eve from a rib—or even a stone (Matthew 3:9)! But the point of the passage is the organic spiritual connection between male and female. Adam and Eve are meant to be together. As someone well said, the woman was created...

> Not from his head, to rule over him;
> Not from his foot, to be trodden on by him;
> But from his side, to be his equal.

The woman is created to be the man's "helper" (Genesis 2:18). This is no slight; the Lord himself is our helper (Genesis 49:25; Deuteronomy 33:29). In the Bible, women are respected, and marriage is honorable (Hebrews 13:4). It is also far from being one-sided. By New Testament times, the emphasis is on the mutual love between man and wife (1 Corinthians 7:3-5; Ephesians 5:21-33).

Is the Bible Chauvinistic?

Some critics complain that the Bible is unfair toward women. Here are a few practical responses.

- The fifth commandment states, "Honor your father and your mother." In the ancient world, mothers were typically ignored. But in Old Testament law, they were to be cherished.

- Jesus had great friendships with men and women alike. In Luke 8:3 we see many women so enthusiastic about his message that they financially supported his ministry.

- Although the apostle Paul was single, the apostle Peter was a married man. One of Jesus' earliest miracles was to heal Peter's mother-in-law (Mark 1:29-31).

- The first witnesses of the resurrected Jesus were women. The 12 are depicted as slow to believe, even in the presence of strong evidence, but the female witnesses are portrayed as faithful (Matthew 28:9,17).

- About 40 percent of the apostle Paul's personal greetings are to women.

- In the book of Acts, numbers of prominent women are converted. These educated, opinionated women would never have been won to a chauvinistic faith.

- Submission is two-way. The command for all believers to submit to one another regardless of gender (Ephesians 5:21) is not invalidated by marriage. Husbands are to be spiritual leaders, but godly leaders often submit to those they are leading.

Genesis 2:25—Does God endorse public nudity?

Nudist campers are hardly sinless souls inhabiting the Garden of Eden. If not for the flesh, perhaps there would be no problem. But sin is a reality, and clothing is the norm (since Genesis 3). In fact, the Lord himself assisted with clothing the first couple. The Bible offers a safe place where a man and a woman can dispense with clothing—marriage.

Genesis 3:16-24—Why didn't God forgive Adam and Eve in the garden instead of kicking them out?

We must be careful not to confuse forgiving with excusing. We may suffer for our bad choices, but that does not mean God doesn't like us anymore or that he hasn't forgiven us. The Lord is full of grace. God *did* forgive Adam and Eve, but the consequences of their choice (guilt, loss of trust, alienation, having to move) didn't just go away. Adam and Even had shown they could not handle the responsibility. By banning Adam and Eve from the garden, God kept them from eating from the tree of life and living forever in their fallen state (Genesis 3:22-24). God cares so much about us that he intervenes multiple times in Genesis, protecting man from himself.

Genesis 4:1—What does the Bible say about polygamy?

Once in Africa I shared a taxi ride with another Christian man. We began to chat about family, and I quickly realized his own family situation was complex—19 children, as I recall. Thinking he might have been a widower who remarried, I asked him, "Two wives?" He replied yes, but he wasn't remarried—he *presently* had two wives. It felt odd to be sitting with a bigamist who was also a believer. His marriage to two women was legal in his nation, but it wasn't biblical.

God's original plan (one man, one wife, for life) is clearly laid out in Genesis 2 even though it was soon flouted (Genesis 4:19). Polygamy was common in Old Testament times, especially among the powerful, but it never facilitated a happy home life (see Genesis 29–31).

Genesis 4:14-17—Who was Cain afraid of? Who was his wife?

A pretty good case can be made for a substantial population outside the "first family." This case is based on the anthropological evidence and the Bible itself. His wife could have been a sibling (there were sisters—Genesis 5:4), but the text does not naturally read this way.

Genesis 5—Did ancient humans really live for hundreds of years?

We have no paleontological evidence of human beings living for hundreds of years. But we do have significant evidence that ancient readers would have understood the numbers to be symbolic, representing *idealized* ages. Carol A. Hill explains:

> The key to understanding the numbers in Genesis is that, in the Mesopotamian worldview, numbers could have both real (numerical) and sacred (numerological or symbolic) meaning. The Mesopotamians used a sexagesimal (base 60) system of numbers, and the patriarchal ages in Genesis revolve around the sacred numbers 60 and 7. In addition to Mesopotamian sacred numbers, the preferred numbers 3, 7, 12, and 40 are used in both the Old and New Testaments. To take numbers figuratively does not mean that the Bible is not to be taken

literally. It just means that the biblical writer was trying to impart a spiritual or historical truth to the text—one that surpassed the meaning of purely rational numbers.

The important question to ask is: Are Genesis and the record of the patriarchs from Adam to Abraham to be considered mythological or historical? Ironically, by interpreting the numbers of Genesis "literally," Christians have created a mythological world that does not fit with the historical or scientific record…The "literal" (or numerical) view is secular while the "symbolic" (or numerological) view is sacred because that is how the original biblical author(s) intended for it to be. To faithfully interpret Genesis is to be faithful to what it means as it was written, not to what people living in a later age assume or desire it to be. It is also ironic that the mythological world created by many well-intentioned and serious "literal" Christians, based partly on the numbers in Genesis, has caused millions of people to reject the Bible and the truths contained therein.[5]

Genesis 6:3—God says his Spirit will not contend with man for more than 120 years. Why did people live so much longer than that?

Some commentators take the 120 years as a human longevity limit. Others understand this as the time remaining between God's lament and the coming of the flood. If this explanation is right, Noah had a good 100 years in which to construct the ark. Such a view is also supported by many whose ages are reported to have exceeded 120 even after the flood. If, on the other hand, these numbers are symbolic (see the previous question and answer), we may be barking up the wrong tree.

Genesis 6:4—Who were the Nephilim?

The term means "the fallen ones." An unholy union, probably human and angelic, resulted in a serious violation of the cosmic order. Some propose they were a race of giants, the offspring of angels and women. Others suggest they were the sinful seed of Cain, who later resurface as the Canaanites. Note that they were on the earth in the days before the flood—and afterward.

Genesis 6–9—Is there archaeological evidence for a global flood?

There is widespread confirmation that floods have occurred all over the world at different times, but there is no evidence for the entire world being flooded simultaneously.

In fact, a literal interpretation of Genesis 7:19 would require more than five miles of water on top of the present ocean levels (Mt. Everest is currently 29,035 feet high, or 5.5 miles). The earth's diameter is 7926 miles, so the volume of additional amount of water created by such a flood would be more than a billion cubic miles. Imagine a cube of water a 1000 miles by 1000 miles by 1000 miles—three to four times more water than is in all the oceans (322,300,000 cubic miles). Further, with this amount of water in the clouds, atmospheric pressure would approach 1000 pounds per square inch. One's whole body would be flattened as if by a steamroller. Living through the flood would have been easier than living before it! Once the waters had fallen from the sky, decompression would have caused nitrogen narcosis—the bends. Not only that, but it took 2.5 months for 20 feet of water to subside (Genesis 8:6,13-14), so it would have taken more than 300 years for the entire 5.5 miles to drain. Also troubling for literalists, Psalm 148:4 says that the "waters [or floods] above the sky" are still there. Where are they? And why is atmospheric pressure so low? The required supernatural explanation invalidates the natural biblical one.

"Flood geologists" believe major surface geological features of the planet were formed during the deluge. Yet assuming the flood happened in the last six or seven thousand years, we have a problem. Our present mountains were all in place. Fossils, rather than being mixed stratigraphically as one would expect in a global deluge, are predictably found in their respective geological strata. (Note too that the geologic column was worked out by Bible believers *before* the time of Darwin, as was the antiquity of the earth.) Another difficulty with the global flood is that the Bible says the Lord used a strong wind to dry the ground. But would this have been of any avail had the entire surface of the planet been covered with water? When the Red Sea was parted by such a wind (Exodus 14:21), the waters were restrained only temporarily; how much more so if the entire planet had been covered. This too suggests the recollection of a local inundation, long before the final version of the flood story.

In the ancient Near East, the *Epic of Atrahasis* (Tablet III) and the *Gilgamesh Epic* (Tablet XI) contained popular flood stories. The pagan versions are roughly parallel to the biblical account, including a god warning a man, the animals, the birds sent out on reconnaissance, the sacrifice after disembarking from the ark, and quite a few other features. At the same time, there are major points of divergence. In the pagan versions, the flood is an outburst of divine irritation, without any reference to sin or judgment. The protagonist's survival is despite the will of heaven, not because of God's gracious initiative. The Mesopotamian accounts, though of historical value, tell us nothing about God. The Israelites adapted the ancient flood story to become a vehicle for telling the truth about God.

Davis A. Young, an evangelical geologist from Calvin College, sensibly addresses the matter of the extent of the flood.

> I do not consider it a violation of the integrity of the biblical text to suppose that the biblical flood account uses a major Mesopotamian event in order to make vital theological points concerning human depravity, faith, and obedience and divine judgment, grace, and mercy. The evangelical church serves no good end by clinging to failed interpretations of the Bible and refusing to explore new directions. Christian scholars have an obligation to lead the way toward a renewed reverence for God's truth wherever it can be found.[6]

So we see that the traditional interpretation is not necessarily the correct one. Although the Genesis flood was probably limited in scope, the watery judgment on the human race serves as an apt illustration for the coming day of judgment (Matthew 24:37-39; 2 Peter 3:3-7).

Misconceptions About the Flood

- *The animals entered two by two.* This is only partially true. Clean animals entered seven pairs at a time, unclean animals two pairs at a time (Genesis 7:2). The extra clean animals were used for sacrifice.

- *The flood lasted 40 days.* In fact, 150 days is the total length (7:24), and Noah was unable to disembark for more than a year because of the floodwaters (7:11; 8:13-14). Forty days was only the period of intensive rain (7:17).

- *The ark alighted on Mount Ararat.* The Bible says it "came to rest on the mountains of Ararat" (8:4). The specific mountain is unnamed.

- *Every animal species found its way to the ark.* Actually, only domesticated animals are mentioned—those the family of Noah would need in order to continue animal industry and sacrifice. No fish made the journey.

- *The account was new.* The flood story was a rewriting of a current narrative, but with significant theological differences. Unlike the pagan stories, it emphasizes God's holiness, wisdom, grace, love, and justice.

Genesis 8:4—Where is Noah's ark? Did it survive?

Would an ark not have been a valuable commodity? Rather than abandon it, the survivors (or others after them) would surely have been more liable to use the wood for structures, tools, fuel, and so on. Ark sightings of timbers from the original ship on Mount Ararat (altitude 17,000 feet) are surely exaggerated. Besides, the Bible never says the ark landed on Ararat. Scholars reject these as speculative claims, often promoted for pecuniary purposes.

Genesis 9:6—Is the death penalty biblical?

Genesis 9:6 specified the death penalty for murder. Yet while the New Testament recognizes that governments enforce capital punishment, it also calls believers not to conform to the patterns of the world (see Romans 12:14–13:7). It is difficult to build a New Testament doctrine on an Old Testament law. The same code that stipulates execution for murder also requires execution for adultery. The list of capital crimes also includes assaulting one's parents, bestiality, blasphemy, bull goring, contempt of court, cursing one's parents, being a rebellious son, female promiscuity, idolatry, incest, kidnapping, being a malicious witness in a capital case, manslaughter, priestly arrogation, Sabbath breaking, sodomy, and sorcery. (These penalties are found mainly in Exodus 21–22; Leviticus 20 and 24; Numbers 15; and Deuteronomy 13; 17; 19; 21–22; and 24). Where do we draw the line? Why favor a death penalty for murder while relinquishing the death penalty for other crimes?

The church of the first three centuries opposed capital punishment. Consider these remarks from respected leaders in the early church.

- "How can we put anyone to death?" (Athenagoras, c. 175).

- "Christians do not attack their assailants in return, for it is not lawful for the innocent to kill even the guilty" (Cyprian, c. 250).

- "It is always unlawful to put a man to death, whom God willed to be a sacred creature" (Lactantius, c. 304–313).

One further comment is in order. An odd double irony characterizes both advocates and opponents of the death penalty. The same people who are pro-life (against killing a fetus) are usually anti-life when it comes to certain criminals. Conversely, the pro-choice advocates (in favor of terminating a fetus) are generally pro-life vis-à-vis crime and punishment. Men and women of faith would do well to think through their position and reach a consistent position.

Genesis 9:25—What is the curse of Ham?

Noah drank too much and passed out. Ham looked upon (leering?) his father Noah's nakedness, and when Noah awoke, he cursed Canaan, Ham's son. Incredibly, some people have argued that this curse is the reason for dark skin on the colored races (Indian, Mongolian, Negro, Melanesian…) and that it explains their economic struggles. This degrading argument has been leveled against many minority groups and is as diabolical as it is fallacious.

Canaan was cursed, not Ham. Ham's descendants are not various races of color, but (transparently) the Canaanites. Genesis 9:18 names Canaan as the ancestor of the Canaanites, whom God said to extirpate from the promised land.

"Curse of Ham" proponents presume Jesus was white. Yet this is absurd because people in the Near East have a dark complexion. The curse of Ham is to be rejected as a pseudobiblical and racist argument.

Genesis 11:3-5—Is there archaeological evidence for the Tower of Babel?

In all likelihood, this was one of the ziggurats (stepped pyramids) discovered at Babylon, perhaps the great stepped pyramid of Etemenanki. Ziggurats were topped with temples—like the Tower of Shechem in Judges 9:46. Some 30 ziggurats have been unearthed in the ancient Near East.

Enuma Elish, the creation account by the Babylonians, ends with the construction of the temple of Marduk, a parallel with the Genesis account (Genesis 1–11). Babylonian religion was heavily focused on astrology, and this passage is one of the Genesis writer's assaults on such idolatry. Indeed, the implications of the many allusions to paganism in the pages of Genesis are easily overlooked by the modern Western reader.

Genesis 14:18—Was Melchizedek a preincarnate appearance of Christ?

The Bible never equates Jesus with Melchizedek, though parallels do exist, as we see in Hebrews 5:6,10; 6:20; and especially 7:1-17. Melchizedek was a priest as well as a royal figure—just like Jesus. Melchizedek's priesthood—and this is the main point the Hebrew writer makes—stood outside the usual order of things. If Jesus were a regular Jewish priest, he would be required to be from the tribe of Levi, but he was from Judah. Melchizedek provides a precedent for a legitimate priesthood prior to and outside the order established under the Jewish Law.

Melchizedek is indeed a fascinating figure, about whom we read only in Genesis, Psalm 110, and Hebrews. To begin with, he was not in the Levitical or Aaronic priesthood because Levi and Aaron were not yet born. "Without father or mother" (Hebrews 7:3) does not mean he was miraculously born (although Melchizedek legends arose through this misunderstanding) but that his priesthood was not supported by any genealogical records.

Psalm 110 indicates the Messiah was indeed to serve in the order of Melchizedek—that is, outside the establishment, the temple system. He was to minister as king, priest, and judge (verses 1,4, and 6). The aim of the writer of Hebrews is not to wow us with the person of Melchizedek, but to provide a precedent for the exceptional person of Jesus Christ. Christ was descended from the tribe of Judah, not Levi, and his heavenly priesthood was incomprehensible to the Old Testament Jews. In Melchizedek the Hebrew writer finds the perfect precedent.

If Melchizedek was greater than Abraham, he was also greater than Levi because Levi was Abraham's great grandson. So if Jesus serves in the order of Melchizedek, he has no need to be a Levite in order to offer sacrifice for our sins. His priesthood is precedented, legitimate, and preeminent.

YOUR BIBLE QUESTIONS ANSWERED

Genesis 16:1-4—Why does Sarah tell Abraham to sleep with their servant Hagar?

This unusual custom was common in its day. Hagar became Abraham's secondary wife, yet Sarah was the legal mother of Hagar's offspring. Notice that Abraham's sleeping with Hagar was Sarah's idea, and in his acquiescence, Abraham too wavered in faith regarding the Lord's promise (Genesis 15:2-4; 17:18-19; 30:3-5). This action was not directly commended by the Lord and led to considerable family hardship, as is the norm when we step outside the moral will of God.

Genesis 16:12—Are Muslims descendants of Ishmael, Abraham's first son?

All Muslims claim Abraham as a spiritual ancestor. Yet the claim that they are descended through Ishmael, Abraham's older son, was fabricated after the time of Muhammad (AD 570–632). In the Qur'an, Abraham sacrifices an unnamed son (Sura 37). The tradition that it was Ishmael and not Isaac came later. The tradition evolved in order to distinguish the Muslims from the two other monotheistic faiths descended from Abraham. This also means that Genesis 16:12 is unfairly applied to the Muslims. The text reads, "He will be a wild donkey of a man; his hand will be against everyone and everyone's hand against him, and he will live in hostility toward all his brothers." This prophecy refers to Ishmael and his seed, not the Islamic peoples.

Genesis 18:1-15—Did Christ appear in the Old Testament?

This interpretation of such passages as Genesis 18:1-15; 22:11; Joshua 5:13-15; and Daniel 3:25 has been popular since the second century. Yet nowhere does the Bible identify any of these theophanies as messianic. Further, in Hebrews 1 the writer argues that Jesus is superior to the angels. But if he *is* an angel…you see the difficulty. And what about the Incarnation? If Jesus came to the earth *before* his first coming, theologians have a lot to untangle. Many interpreters think differently, and I certainly respect their opinions. My current position is that despite the temptations to see Christ in these angel appearances, we should be cautious about reading more into the record than is there.

Genesis 20:3-5—Abraham pretends Sarah is his sister, but God is angry with Abimelech. Why?

The Bible tells the stories of its characters without whitewashing. Abraham's faith weakens, and he tells a lie (or a half-truth, as Sarah was technically his half sister). As a result, he is rebuked by the pagan king's behavior. Sometimes nonbelievers appear more righteous than believers.

As for Abimelech's innocence, he was on the verge of marrying a woman who already had a husband. A clear conscience does not mean innocence (1 Corinthians 4:4). Had Abimelech spent much time getting to know Sarah, he would have soon discovered the truth about his latest acquisition. Incidentally, Sarah was a ripe 90 years of age at this time, and some mock at the notion that she could have been taken into a harem. Yet beauty is in the eye of the beholder. Considering such factors as charm, class, and wisdom, who is to say Abimelech didn't find her an attractive addition to the harem of Gerar?

Genesis 32:22-30—Did Jacob really see God?

This does seem to contradict John 1:18, which says no one has ever seen God. Often the Bible describes God's interaction with man anthropomorphically. That is, it describes things in human terms: seeing, remembering, relenting, and so on. For example, Exodus 33:11 pictures the Lord speaking to Moses face-to-face. Sinful man cannot see God in his full glory and purity and brilliance without being vaporized (Habakkuk 1:13). Yet Jacob did see God, in some sense, even if it was only the Lord's representative (an angel). Further, he "saw" what happens when people try to extort blessings from the hand of the Lord. He "saw" that no one can, by sheer grit, back God into a corner, force his hand, or extract blessings. He "saw" his own weakness and felt it painfully. Perhaps Jacob did see God—it all depends on how you define the word *see*.

Even to catch a sideward glimpse of God would be suffocating, enervating, totally debilitating (Daniel 10:17). No one has ever seen God in one sense, but we all see him in another sense. The fullness of what makes God who he is becomes visible in Jesus Christ. Only in Jesus do we behold God (John 1:14,18; 14:9). Yet when we see Christ, we are not overwhelmed with the awesome, terrifying, incinerating presence of God. We find an ally, an advocate, a brother, a friend.

Genesis 38:8-10—Is God opposed to birth control?

Onan sinned by refusing to fulfill his duty to his brother and provide an heir (Deuteronomy 25:5-10). The passage has nothing to do with birth control, though the church has traditionally used it as a proof text. As long as no conception has taken place, the ethical issues of birth control are simple. Things get more complex when an egg has been fertilized—which was not the situation with Onan.

5

Exodus to Deuteronomy

Exodus 1:7—Seventy persons from Jacob's family entered Egypt, and hundreds of thousands left. Is this likely?

There is abundant evidence that noble Egyptians had servants—and Semitic servants at that. As economic assets, servants were expected to reproduce, so the growth of the embryonic nation is plausible. On psychological grounds, the invention of such a story is exceedingly improbable. If you are cutting a national lineage out of whole cloth, why concoct slave origins? Why not invent a more honorable pedigree? This attests strongly to the veracity of the account. For more on the population of the nation and the size of its army, see the entry for Numbers 1:46.

Exodus 1:1—Who was Pharaoh? Was there more than one Pharaoh?

Pharaoh is the generic name for the king of Egypt, especially in use by the time of the New Kingdom (1550 BC onward). The word means "great house" and originally referred to the royal palace. There were many pharaohs—in fact, more than 30 dynasties of them, spanning the better part of three millennia.

Exodus 2:18—Was Moses' father-in-law named Reuel or Jethro?

Reuel is another name for Jethro (Exodus 3:1; 18:1). Then as now, people sometimes had more than one name.

Exodus 4:24—Why did God threaten to kill Moses? Or was it Moses' son?

The Hebrew pronoun is ambivalent: God was going to kill "him." Following the threat to kill the firstborn sons of Egypt in verse 23, the referent could well be Moses' son. Yet presumably Moses himself is the one in trouble for ignoring the circumcision command, already centuries old and dating to the time of Abraham (Genesis 17:9-14). Moses should have circumcised his son on the eighth day. Whether Moses himself or his son was in imminent danger does not matter. God's command was to be obeyed. Zipporah, Moses' wife, is somewhat scornful of God's requirement. After she circumcises their son, God leaves them alone.

Exodus 6:3—Is God's name Jehovah or Yahweh?

The Jews have been loath to pronounce or write God's covenant name, *Yahweh*. (They often write *G-d*.) The *tetragrammaton* (Greek for "four-lettered") refers to the four consonants that make up the word *God* in the Hebrew Bible: *YHWH*. To avoid taking the Lord's name in vain, scribes supplied the vowels from the Hebrew word *Adonai* (Lord), which are *a-o-a*. Put together, the word appeared to be pronounced YeHoWaH, or Jehovah.

This is a misnomer. The Bible never calls God *Jehovah*. Scholars posit that the original pronunciation was *Yahweh*. Modern English Bibles usually represent the tetragrammaton by the word LORD (with initial cap and small caps). At any rate, *Jehovah* is a mispronunciation of the Hebrew, so it is laughable when one is adamant about a particular pronunciation and then fails so miserably to get it right. It is not necessary to say *Yahweh*, but to do so is not misguided.

Exodus 7:13—Did God override Pharaoh's free will and harden his heart? Was that fair?

Some passages say that God hardened Pharaoh's heart, others say that Pharaoh hardened his own heart, and still others stress both aspects. These hardenings seem to occur simultaneously. Sun hardens clay but melts butter—but not because the sun favors one over the other. Rather, each responds to the heat according to its own nature. Two factors determine the outcome: the action or energy applied to the substance and the substance itself.

Technically, the verb *to be hardened* occurs only once, in 7:3. Pharaoh and God appear to alternately cause the hardening, but Pharaoh was the one in control. The Hebrew uses the verb *to be made strong* in about half of the cases and *to be made heavy* in many of the remaining instances. Pharaoh's heart *is* hard in 7:13-14,22; 8:19; 9:17,35. He hardens it himself in 8:15,32; 9:34, and God hardens it in 4:21; 7:3; 9:12; 10:1,20,27; 11:10; 14:4,8. The alternation is only one of description.

God applied the pressure, and Pharaoh responded. But unlike butter and clay, Pharaoh had free will in responding to God, so he was ultimately accountable for his response. God is fair, and his laws apply equally to all. God is sovereign and omniscient, but his power and knowledge never compel us to do wrong. In him there is no injustice. We react to God's influence according to our nature. Are we hardhearted and stubborn? If so, the circumstances of life (the things God sends our way) can stiffen us. Are we softhearted and humble? Then we tend to listen and respond well to spiritual input.

Exodus 12:37-38—When was the Exodus?

Scholars place the Exodus sometime between 1500 and 1200 BC, conservatives sometimes favoring the earlier period. At face value,

1 Kings 6:1 (see the question and answer below) indicates it occurred in 1446 BC (480 years before 966 BC, when the temple was constructed). I have some sympathy for the traditional date of 1446 BC but believe the archaeological data better support 1290 BC. (See "What do we mean when we say the Bible is inspired?" on pages 13-14.)

Exodus 12:37-38—Did Egyptian historians mention the Exodus?

No. The Egyptians recorded what they wanted to record, and like many modern regimes, they avoided bad press. As a rule, ancient civilizations manipulated the media and never recorded anything shameful or disgraceful. Further, plenty of Egyptian records mention slavery of foreigners (and Semitic peoples in particular).

Exodus 13:18—Are the Red Sea and the Sea of Reeds the same?

The Hebrew reads *Sea of Reeds*, but the Septuagint (the Greek translation from the third century BC) and the Greek New Testament use *Red Sea*. This is not a contradiction. In ancient times the entire area was wetter, and the Sea of Reeds, *Yam Suph*, was larger than at present. Because the Sea of Reeds and the Red Sea were connected, some ancients referred to both as the Red Sea. So it isn't inaccurate to call *Yam Suph* the Red Sea because one is, in a sense, part of the other.

Exodus 14:21—Was the Red Sea parted by a volcanic explosion on the Aegean island of Thera?

This intriguing and much-celebrated idea explains too much. Supposedly the force of the eruption caused the ten plagues and then parted the Red Sea. God could have used natural means to deliver his people, yet the Exodus account reads more like a series of true miracles. One gets the feeling that this conjecture nearly removes God from the picture. Moreover, the eruption of Thera took place in the wrong century—before 1600 BC. The Exodus took place in the thirteenth or fifteenth century.

Exodus 20:1—Is the Torah different from the Law of Moses?

The Law of Moses consists loosely of the books of Genesis through Deuteronomy. The Jews call it the Torah (law or instruction), which strictly speaking applies to the laws beginning in Exodus 20. Another name is the Pentateuch (the five rolls). The Torah called the people of God to faithful covenant living, into a relationship with the living God. Moses received the Law on Mount Sinai shortly after the exodus from Egyptian slavery. Though the Ten Commandments are the nucleus of the Torah, other laws followed. Rabbis eventually counted 613 commandments (248 positive rules and 365 prohibitions), though this number is debatable.

Exodus 20:1-17—Why were there two tablets?

Covenants were normally produced in duplicate—identical copies for each party. In this case, one copy was Israel's, another God's. The Lord had Israel retain his copy. The Ten Commandments are also referred to as the Decalogue, the "ten words" (Exodus 20:1-17; 21:1–23:14; Deuteronomy 5:6-21).

Exodus 20:8-11—What is the purpose of the Sabbath? And why don't we worship on Saturday?

The Bible teaches that we are to worship every day, not just one in seven (Romans 12:1). The Sabbath extends from sundown Friday to sundown Saturday. But Christians are never commanded to observe the Sabbath. In fact, just the opposite (Romans 14:5-6; Galatians 4:8-11; Colossians 2:16-18; Hebrews 4:9). No one fully keeps the Sabbath today, for that would entail observing not only the seventh day but also Sabbatical and Jubilee Years (Leviticus 25)—no work, cancelation of debts, and so forth. With separation of church and state under the new covenant, a full implementation of the biblical Sabbath is impossible.

The early church used Sabbaths for evangelistic purposes, knowing that they would find seekers in the synagogues. The main meeting day for Christians was Sunday, not Saturday (Acts 20:7; 1 Corinthians 16:2). In ancient times, Sunday was a workday, and so (in the early second century, at least) the disciples met at dawn and again in the evening on Sunday. A Sunday Sabbath finds its way into Christianity only after two centuries. Consider the testimony of two early second-century writers, Ignatius and "Barnabas" (author of the Epistle of Barnabas). Both interpret the Sabbath as a Jewish legal requirement no longer binding on Christians.

> If, then, those who had lived in antiquated practices came to newness of hope, no longer keeping the Sabbath but living in accordance with the Lord's Day [Sunday], on which our life also arose through him and his death (which some deny)... (Ignatius, *Magnesians* 9:1).

> Finally, he says to them, "I cannot bear your new moons and Sabbaths." You see what he means: "It is not the present Sabbaths that are acceptable to me, but the one that I have made; on that Sabbath, after I have set everything at rest, I will create the beginning of an eighth day, which is the beginning of another world." This is why we spend the eighth day in celebration, the day on which Jesus both arose from the dead and, after appearing again, ascended into heaven (Epistle of Barnabas 15:8-9).

Torah-observing Jews teach that *Shabbat* is for the purpose of what many Christians call a "quiet time." Prayer and study of the word (especially the Torah) are to dominate the day. As the Jerusalem Talmud has it, "The Sabbaths were given to Israel in order that they might study Torah" (Shabbat 15:3). Many Jews make this quality family time, even opening their homes to non-Jews. Putting it all together, Shabbat is rest but not laziness. It is devotion to God but not work. It is for study and prayer, but it is not to be a burden. And for those with families, it is a time to share.

Exodus 20:13—Does the command not to murder pertain to all killing?

The original text has *ratsach* (to murder). *Harag* (to kill) is not used in this verse, and so the NIV translators' decision against a footnote is well grounded. In the Torah, some forms of killing were authorized by God, even in the books of Exodus and Deuteronomy. Those that were not constituted murder.

Exodus 21:10-11—Are there grounds for divorce other than adultery?

Divorce undoes the plan of God (Genesis 2:24), but sometimes it appears to be unavoidable. Grounds in the Jewish Law included failure on the part of the husband to provide food, clothing, and marital rights. That is, he was to meet his wife's physical and emotional needs. Further, Paul recognizes adultery and abandonment as grounds for leaving a marriage relationship (1 Corinthians 7:15).

Exodus 21:22—Do any Bible passages relate to the morality of the morning-after pill?

The morning-after pill is an abortifacient, with one exception. Taken a few days before conception, it is just a contraceptive. Would that the discussion were so simple.

No Scriptures address the subject head-on. This is curious because abortion and exposure of unwanted infants were common in the ancient world. Various poisons were administered to induce abortions. At that time, the Hippocratic Oath forbade abortions. The closest the Bible comes to addressing the issue is in this passage, where the penalty for causing an abortion or miscarriage was a fine, not the death penalty, as if the baby were already born. Although I am not proabortion, I do admit that the Bible recognizes *some* differences between a baby already born and one still in the womb.

Most Bible students believe life starts at conception, based on the poetry of Job 10:8-12; Psalm 139:13-16; and Jeremiah 1:5. But did God intend poems to be mined for doctrine? The following questions need to be answered honestly.

- The fertilization process requires many hours and is followed by another day in which the individual (diploid) is formed. In what sense is the mother-to-be pregnant before the process is complete?

- Is the loss of a 16-cell embryo equal to the loss of a full-term fetus?

- Up until two weeks, the zygote can split into twins, triplets, and so on. The process of individuation is still incomplete. Can a soul be shared three ways?

- The baby's heart starts beating after 22 days. Does life begin with the heartbeat?

- The sex of the embryo is not determined until the seventh week. Accordingly, many Muslims and Jews consider the embryo to be fully human only after 40 days. Do Jews and Muslims value life less than Christians?

- Recognizable EEG patterns (the mental activity associated with humanity) don't appear until 24 weeks. What are the implications? Is it possible that the individual becomes fully human on a continuum?

- Continuous brainwaves do not begin until about 28 weeks. Until then, the neurons carrying pain impulses to the brain are not yet fully wired. What are the implications?

- Is abortion allowable if this is the only way to save the mother's life?

Whatever believers think about this important subject should be informed by science and theology and should be moderated by conscience. Antiabortionists are inconsistent when they are pro-life in regard to an embryo or fetus but anti-life when calling for the execution of the abortionist. On the other side, abortionists are inconsistent when they affirm that a fetus is fully human *and* that it's at the mother's disposal (as part of her body). Is it human, or not? If it's a baby before it's born, it must not be cast off. Otherwise, on what grounds could eliminating a one-year-old baby be rejected as murder? Doublethink has moral consequences.

Exodus 25:10—What happened to the ark of the covenant after Solomon's reign?

The Ethiopians claim to have it but will not allow the outside world access. In *Raiders of the Lost Ark,* it is stored away in a wooden box amid thousands of other boxes in a massive warehouse. But 2 Kings 24:13 suggests the Babylonians captured it. The ark was a plain wooden box (Exodus 37:1) once the gold was stripped off. Maybe the wood was burned in the fires set by Nebuchadnezzar's armies in 587 BC. Wood doesn't normally survive from antiquity. Probably the best answer is that it doesn't matter (see Jeremiah 3:16).

By the way, the Hebrew word for *ark* here is not the same as that for Noah's ark (Genesis 6:14-16). *Chest* would have been a better translation.

Exodus 25:10—How long is a cubit?

The cubit was a common measure of length. Although scholars are still discussing its exact length, it likely originated as the length of a man's forearm, from the elbow (Latin: *cubitum*) to the tip of his middle finger. It seems the "common cubit" was 18 inches (46 centimeters, or half a meter). Judges 3:16 says Ehud's short sword is a cubit long. Noah's ark was 300 cubits long (450 feet, or 137 meters). Goliath, at 6 cubits and a span (4 inches), was 9 feet 4 inches. If the "short cubit" (15 inches) is in view, then he was somewhere around 7 feet 10 inches. The "royal cubit" was 20 inches (51 centimeters), and the "long cubit" measured 22 inches (56 centimeters). For a rough conversion from cubits to feet, multiply by 1.5; from meters, divide by 2.

YOUR BIBLE QUESTIONS ANSWERED

Exodus 28:33-35—When the high priest entered the Most Holy Place, did he wear these bells so the people outside would know he was still alive?

No, I don't think so. The passage does mention the danger of entering the Holy Place before the Lord, but the function of the bells is difficult to discern. By the first century AD, some Jews believed the bells stood for thunder.

> When [the high priest] officiated, he had on...a blue garment, round, without seam, with fringework, and reaching to the feet. There were also golden bells that hung upon the fringes, and pomegranates intermixed among them. The bells signified thunder, and the pomegranates lightning (Josephus, *War* 5.5.7).

People sometimes say the high priest also tied a rope to his ankle so he could be pulled out if things went poorly. The Bible mentions no rope. Who knows—this may be true, but it is currently mere speculation.

Exodus 34:1-28—Is it a coincidence there are ten commandments in Exodus 34, just like the Ten Commandments of Exodus 20?

Sometimes the Exodus 34 list is called the Ritual Decalogue, and the list in chapter 20 is called the Ethical Decalogue. After the earlier giving of the law at Sinai, along with its amplification in the chapters following Exodus 20, Israel had lapsed into gross idolatry (chapter 32). Chapter 34 is a sort of renewal of the covenant, a severe warning against returning to the temptations of Canaanite idolatry.

This section of Exodus deliberately imitates the original Decalogue. Ten words of warning urge moral, doctrinal, and religious purity in undivided devotion to Yahweh. Thus, this second edition of the covenant serves a triple function: a rebuke after the idolatrous incident with the golden calf, a recap of God's distinctive covenant requirements, and a reminder to holy living, which anticipates Leviticus in its gravity and specificity.

Leviticus 1:2—Why would God tell people to slaughter defenseless animals for sacrifice?

The biblical answer is that sin requires a sacrifice of innocent blood. We do not sin in a vacuum. Our sin hurts God (Psalm 51:4) and cost Jesus his life (Acts 2:23; 2 Corinthians 5:21). Yet this crucial message increasingly falls on deaf ears for several reasons.

- As the world rejects the God of the Bible, it also minimizes the radical difference between mankind and other animals. This works both ways—it dehumanizes us as humans, and it personifies much of the animal kingdom. Through cartoons and the media, animal sentimentality levels are elevated.

- We easily project ideas of human love onto the animal kingdom. If we should refrain from eating cows (whether today or under the Levitical sacrificial system), why not refrain from killing carrots? Where does one draw the line? Are lambs really innocent, or are they guilty? Animals are not subject to moral categories. Does the lioness feel remorse for taking down a defenseless gazelle? When a mosquito drinks our blood, has it transgressed a moral boundary? Of course not.

- Increasingly, sin and crime are regarded in terms of sickness. This decreases human responsibility.

- Our society overprotects us from death, both human and animal. Consequently, we overreact when we contemplate animal death.

Leviticus 4:2,13,22,27—Why does the Law provide forgiveness only for unintentional sins?

As the writer of Hebrews remarked, animal sacrifices could never remove sin; they could only remind us of our guilt (Hebrews 10:1-4). Yet all sins, unintentional as well as intentional, can be forgiven in Christ—whose sacrifice the entire old covenant system anticipates.

Leviticus 7:22,26—Do the prohibitions about eating fat and drinking blood still apply to us?

According to Jesus, the kosher code no longer applies (Mark 7:19), though at times we ought to moderate our diet out of respect for others (Acts 15:29). That is not to say that such unhealthy practices are commended (be warned, lovers of blood pudding)!

Leviticus 10:1-7—Why were Nadab and Abihu killed?

The text says they offered unauthorized fire. Verse 8 implies that they were inebriated. For whatever reason, they disobeyed the clear word of God.

Leviticus 11—What does *kosher* mean?

The kosher laws, or *kashrut*, are the dietary regulations of Leviticus 11 and Deuteronomy 14. Infractions made one ritually unclean. Not all forbidden foods were unhygienic.

Leviticus 11:6,19—Leviticus 11 says a rabbit chews the cud, but the rabbit is not a ruminant. Also, bats seem to be incorrectly grouped with the birds. Is the Bible mistaken?

Rabbits practice refection, which resembles chewing the cud. And the Bible makes no claim to zoological precision, so this is only a surface contradiction. As for the bat, the food laws covered a number of unclean flying animals, such as herons, hawks, storks, and owls. Since a bat looks like a bird, it is included in the same list.

Consider Peter's vision in Acts 10:12, where we read of "four-footed animals, as well as reptiles of the earth and birds of the air." Notice the classification. Most mammals are tetrapods and fall into the first category. But some reptiles are four-footed (lizards, skinks, crocodiles). To criticize an ancient religious text for not being scientific would be unfair. The meaning is perfectly clear. See "What do we mean when we say the Bible is inspired?" on pages 13-14.

Leviticus 18:21—If God hates child sacrifice, why did he sacrifice his Son for us?

The crucifixion is very different from child sacrifice.

- Jesus was God's Son, but he was not a helpless victim. He voluntarily submitted his will to the Father's will (Matthew 26:52-54; John 18:11).

- The death of Christ is consistently portrayed as *self*-sacrifice (John 10:17-18).

- Ancient pagans believed that giving up their firstborn, like offering firstfruits, was essential to agriculture and fertility. Canaanite religions revolved around weather and farming. Jesus' death, however, brought no such temporal benefit. The deaths of multitudes of babies in ancient times (for example, the sacrifices to Molech) were made by men to a false (nonexistent) god. Shockingly, child sacrifice continues in some parts of the world even today.

- The crucifixion of Jesus Christ was more than the death of a man; it was the experience of death, in some sense, by God. Acts 20:28 says that God bought the church with his own blood. No human could ever die for the sins of another (Psalm 49:7-8). In this vital respect, the death of Jesus was unlike any sacrifice in history.

- Finally, as a matter of interest, the death of Jesus was foreshadowed by Isaac on Mount Moriah (Genesis 22). Neither was ultimately lost: Isaac was saved by a substitution, and Jesus was rescued through resurrection, having "substituted" for us on the cross. God does not desire the destruction of a child.

Leviticus 19:28—Are tattoos sinful?

Tattoos associated with idolatry were apparently common among

Canaanites and other peoples. God had religious reasons for forbidding the Jews to put marks on their bodies. Today, unless tattoos have pagan religious significance, the biblical restriction does not directly apply.

Of course, one should note hygienic, cultural, relational, aesthetic, and other considerations before getting a tattoo.

Leviticus 20:1-5—Who is Molech? What other gods did people worship in Canaan?

Molech was one of the most important gods in Canaan, and the Israelites were often attracted to him. He was the Ammonite god of the underworld, to whom firstborn children were sacrificed alive as burnt offerings. Here are some of the other popular deities of the day:

- *Ba'al*—A Canaanite vegetation deity and father of seven storm gods. In Israelite history, he was more popular than Yahweh (God). First Kings 18:16-40 contains the big showdown between the prophets of Baal and the prophet Elijah. See also Numbers 25:1-3; Judges 2:10-13; 2 Kings 10:18-28; Jeremiah 2:8,23-25; 7:9-11; 19:5; 23:13; 32:29,35. Baal-Zebub is "Lord of the Flies" (2 Kings 1:2-3,6,16). *Baal* means "lord."

- *Asherah*—Originally Amorite, she was the great mother goddess of fertility and is mentioned in nine books of the Bible. Asherah poles were set up beside altars to Baal and Yahweh (1 Kings 14:22-24).

- *Dagon*—a Philistine divinity (Judges 16:23-30; 1 Samuel 5:2-7; 1 Chronicles 10:10).

- *Chemosh*—a Moabite god (1 Kings 11:7; 2 Kings 23:13).

- *Ashtoreth*—a Sidonian goddess (Judges 2:13; 10:6; 1 Samuel 7:3-4; 12:10; 31:10; 1 Kings 11:5; 2 Kings 23:13).

- Household gods were also popular (Genesis 31:19; Joshua 24:14).

Idolatry was ubiquitous. It proved a perennial struggle for the Israelites.

Leviticus 21:16-23—Why did God prohibit people with special needs from being priests?

Is this sort of discrimination necessarily wrong? The Lord gives strict regulations for the priesthood. Was "ageism" the reason that the Lord had priests retire from service at 50 years of age (Numbers 8:25) or that he excluded young men from the army unless they were at least 20 years old (Numbers 1:3)? Looking at the passage in question, we realize that the manifold pressures of ministering before the Lord did not need to be amplified by the added burdens of physical deformity (such as blindness) or the emotional strain of self-consciousness (as in the case of a dwarf). But this is only a practical line of reasoning.

The reason given in the broader context (chapters 21–22) is that certain things make a person ceremonially unclean, or unsuitable for coming into the sanctuary of God: contact with the dead, nocturnal emission, physical defects, and so on. The animals to be sacrificed must be without blemish, and so must the priests who offer them. Thus the obstacles are actually matters of ritual, not morality or worth. God's ways are not our ways (Isaiah 55:8-9). And yet that does not mean he is at fault for "discriminating." The deformed among the tribe of Levi were still allowed to eat the sacrifices (21:22). In the loving plan of God, they were to be provided for. Nor should we conclude that because they were excluded from officiating in temple cult, they were prohibited from having a meaningful relationship with the Lord. ("Coming near" is a technical term for priestly service.) In this sense, the Lord does not discriminate.

Numbers 1:46—What was ancient Israel's population?

Israel's population was in the millions, but the question is whether the army was really as large as 603,550 at the time of the Exodus. To most scholars this figure seems high, perhaps a retrojection from later times. Note that all tribal totals end in 00 except Gad's, which ends in

ndicate more than mere rounding. Numbers 10:36 men-
ess thousands." The Hebrew word for thousand (*'elef*)
a_ _ _ clan." Perhaps the impressive numbers in the account of
the growth of the Hebrews originate from this meaning of *'elef.* This
would explain why the entire army was deployed against Ai, a city of
barely 5000 men (12,000 total population, Joshua 8:25), or why the
Israelite army numbers only 40,000 in the battle of Jericho (Joshua
4:13). The original exodus population would still have been sizeable,
though the national population did not reach the millions until the
time of the monarchy.

Numbers 1:46—Why are only the males counted in the census?

It was the custom in biblical times to count men only. This convention was followed even in the book of Acts (2:41; 4:4). Yet in Numbers
not even all men are numbered, only those of fighting age. This is ap-
propriate for a military census.

Numbers 11:25—How could the Spirit fall on the elders in Moses' time if the Spirit wasn't yet given (John 7:39)?

John 7 may mean the Spirit wasn't *generally* given in pre-Christian
times, that it came to only a handful of persons. And a distinction may
exist between an external reception of the Spirit and the indwelling of
the new covenant. Before Christ, the Spirit came to a few in a dramatic,
visible, and *external* way (Judges 3:10; 6:34; 11:29; 14:6; 15:14; 1 Samuel
10:10; 11:6; 19:20-23; 2 Kings 2:15; 3:15; 1 Chronicles 12:18; 2 Chronicles 15:1; 20:14; 24:20), just as it falls on a handful in new covenant
times (Acts 8:15-17; 10:44; 11:15). This is not the same as the *internal*
reception (in one's heart) mentioned in John 7:38; Acts 2:38; and Galatians 4:6. Either way, the Lord is God, and he works in different lives
in different ways according to his sovereign purpose.

Numbers 34:3—How did the Dead Sea get its name?

In the Old Testament, the Dead Sea is called the Salt Sea (Genesis

14:3). Oceanic salinity is around 3.5 percent. Yet the Dead Sea has a phenomenally high salt content—around 30 percent. No life can survive; that is why it is called dead. Its surface is nearly 1400 feet below sea level, making it the lowest depression on the face of the earth. By the way, if you decide to go for a swim, prepare for a chemical sting and an exhilarating buoyancy.

Deuteronomy 13:1-5—How can we know whether claims of miracles are legit?

The acid test is congruity with the revealed word of God. The Lord could possibly be testing us, even when a sign appears to be genuine, according to Deuteronomy 13. People of faith may be susceptible of gullibility (Matthew 10:16; Luke 16:8). For more, see the entry for 2 Thessalonians 2:9-11.

Deuteronomy 15:4,11—Verse 4 says there will be no more poor people in Israel, and verse 11 says there will always be poor people in the land. Why?

The Bible is both an idealistic and a realistic book. The ideal is that all share and share alike, but in reality, poverty will prove to be a pervasive problem. Jesus reiterated this truth (Mark 14:7).

Deuteronomy 15:12-18—Does the Bible condone slavery?

To begin with, in Old Testament times, when the people of God governed themselves, the Law of Moses regulated this institution; it did not idealize it. In New Testament times, when the Romans ruled, the church did not encourage slavery, but it did work with the socioeconomic reality of slavery. True enough, slavers in later times quoted the Scriptures to support their inhumane practices. Yet as we will see, American chattel slavery—the sort of slavery most of us are familiar with—was very different from slavery in the ancient world. Further, there was a level of human rights in the Scriptures unique in the ancient world.

First, a few points about slavery in the Roman world.

- It was not racially based. Only one's clothing indicated his status as a slave, not the color of his skin!

- Slavery was not socially based. Slaves were not necessarily the lowest rung of society. Some slaves owned property, led a normal family life, and sometimes even participated in the same clubs as their masters.

- Slavery did not necessarily entail menial positions. Some slaves worked in the civil service, others as doctors, nurses, accountants, or writers. Famous ex-slaves included Governor Felix (Acts 23–24), Aesop (fifth century BC), and Saint Patrick (fifth century AD).

- Slaves were often freed, especially as their labor was cheaper when the master wasn't footing the bill for the slave's room and board.

- Persons sold themselves into slavery in order to repay debts. In other words, slavery might be voluntary and temporary.

Hebrew servitude was a vast improvement over slavery in the outside world.

- There were anti-kidnapping laws (Exodus 21:16), which meant that most slaves became slaves because of poverty or warfare.

- There were strict anti-harm laws. A master who hurt his slave was to be prosecuted (Exodus 21:20,26). No other ancient law holds a master accountable for treatment of his slave. The Code of Hammurabi permitted a master to slice off disobedient slave's ear. In contrast, under Mosaic Law, a slave was to be set free if his master knocked a tooth out.

- There were laws in favor of the poor, including automatic debt cancelation (Leviticus 25:8-55) and gleaning laws (Leviticus 19:9).

- Hebrew slaves were to be freed in the seventh year, though with the option to make the slave relationship permanent (Exodus 21:2-5). Laws for foreign slaves were less stringent, but still Israel was commanded to love the stranger in the land (Leviticus 19:33-34).

The New Testament moved mankind even closer to God's standard.

- The slave trade is condemned in 1 Timothy 1:10 (see also Revelation 18:13).

- Master–slave relations were addressed in the light of the cross (Ephesians 6:9; Colossians 4:1).

- Status in Christ did not depend on socioeconomic factors (Galatians 3:28; Colossians 3:11).

- Nowhere are masters told to demand submission from their slaves (1 Timothy 6:1-2).

- It is anachronistic of us to fault Paul and other early Christians for not stirring up dissension. The Roman Empire was not a democracy, and slave revolts were always brutally crushed.

In the early church slaves were treated with dignity.

- They often occupied positions of leadership.

- According to Clement (1 Clement 55:2, about AD 96), some Christians sold themselves into slavery in order to free others.

- Many slaves were attracted to the Christian faith. Why would they do this if (as some critics allege) Christianity put them down? They did it for the same reason that minorities and women were attracted: They were respected, welcomed, loved, and honored.

A few final thoughts:

- Through the course of biblical history, an ethic of dignity and respect was cultivated. God was enlightening his people more and more through the course of biblical history.

- It must be emphasized that there is a difference between recording and approving. The Bible did not actively encourage the slave trade.

- Slavery in New Testament times was radically different from slavery in the more recent American experience.

- Most criticisms of slavery in the Bible are based on caricatures of Christianity, ignorance of Hebraic law, and lack of exposure to the true message of the gospel.

- Those who labored for emancipation, especially in Britain and the United States, were inspired by biblical principles. Through Christian influence, slavery was eventually eliminated in most of the world. This did *not* take place because of the influence of Hinduism, or Islam, or any other major world religion. Amen!!

Deuteronomy 16:16—Did Israelites go to church just three times a year?

Yes, in effect. Only the men were required to go for the feasts of Passover, Pentecost, and Tabernacles. Women were welcome, but to allow for domestic responsibilities, they were not under pressure to attend. This is not to say there were only three corporate gatherings annually, for there were many, in addition to religious observances in the home. Yet only three were mandatory.

Deuteronomy 20:16—Why does God command Israel to be so violent?

Canaanite sin commonly included child sacrifice, male and female temple prostitution, incest, and more (Leviticus 18.) This was a heart-less society, and the Lord knew that its influence on Israel would be sufficient to drag the new nation into spiritual darkness. In fact, this is exactly what eventually happened in the book of Judges. Israelites only partially broke away from "the world." They even intermarried with the Canaanites and other pagan nations, as we see in Ezra and Nehemiah. God had given the Canaanites time to turn from their ways (Genesis 15:16), but they eventually proved they were beyond reforming.

Deuteronomy 20 contains important instructions on Israel's political approach to other pagan cities. Notice the sharp distinction between the Canaanites and the surrounding nations. There was to be no relationship with the Canaanites, but other nations were to be offered terms of peace. Under the new covenant, the rules change; the bar is raised. See the entry for Matthew 5:44.

[handwritten annotation: Same as the "Amorites"]

Deuteronomy 20:18-19—What does the Bible teach about illegal aliens?

God's commands for Israel's national life are not to be applied verbatim to other countries, such as America. But perhaps we can apply some timeless biblical truths to this question.

We are called to obey the laws of the land (Romans 13:1-7). America is peculiar in that it is a nation built of immigrants, as the inscription on the Statue of Liberty affirms:

> Give me your tired, your poor,
> Your huddled masses, yearning to breathe free,
> The wretched refuse of your teeming shore.
> Send these, the homeless, tempest-tossed to me.
> I lift my lamp beside the golden door!

Inflexible policies are rarely in harmony with the principle of love. The Bible calls us to love the alien (Leviticus 19:34) because God loves the alien (Deuteronomy 10:18-19).

On the other hand, illegal aliens should move toward lawful status.

Lying to immigration authorities can damage one's conscience, and always being on the run can erode faith. Social services are expensive, and some needs are more legitimate than others. The best option for illegal aliens may be to come clean, plead for clemency, and let God move in his own way. In some cases, going back to countries of origin is unrealistic or even dangerous (for example, because of political or religious persecution).

The church is not to be vigilantes who cause trouble or hardship for those who, for whatever reasons, have chosen to hide from immigration authorities. Let's balance justice with compassion. When dealing with individuals, we should probably consider each situation on a case-by-case basis.

Deuteronomy 21:18-21—How could God command people to kill disobedient sons?

The covenant community was also a political unit. Israel was not a democracy; it was to be a true theocracy, so there was no separation of church and state. Also, the rebellious son was not a child, and his transgressions were "adult sins"—drunkenness, a decadent lifestyle, refusal to listen to authority figures in his life, and the like. The Old Testament nation had the responsibility to police itself. This was never intended to be applied in Christian times. The Lord had lower standards for his people in Old Testament times than under the Christian covenant, but he is still the same God.

Deuteronomy 22:5—Why shouldn't women wear men's clothing?

Some groups teach that it is a sin for a woman to wear man's clothing and vice versa. The Mosaic Law forbade this in Israel because it was the way of the Canaanites, and God's people were to be separate and distinct. I am not in favor of cross-dressing because it is usually associated with sexual perversion, but the New Testament doesn't explicitly forbid this sort of thing. Old Testament commands normally do not apply to New Testament times unless they are repeated in the New Testament. Besides, through the centuries, clothing styles change drastically. In ancient Rome, men wore skirts.

We do not live under the Law of Moses. Still, from Genesis to Revelation, God's word consistently upholds clear distinctions between the genders. Our society increasingly blurs gender issues to the detriment of the family and insecurity of countless men and women alike.

Deuteronomy 22:28-29—Does the Old Testament forbid premarital sex? And why did rapists get off so easy and women have to marry them?

Genesis 2:24 associates sex with marriage, and extramarital sex is consistently portrayed as contrary to the will of God. Ponder the principles of Proverbs 5–7, compare the sexual restraint of Jacob to that of Shechem (Genesis 29; 34), and note God's white-hot zeal against promiscuity (Number 25:6-8).

As for Deuteronomy 22:28-29, two parties have been wronged— the woman and her family. A high premium was placed on virginity. If the woman had been violated, her chances for a good marriage (to another) were shattered. The regulation in this passage guaranteed her a home and prevented her from being wronged a second time by being discarded. (Consider the wrong Tamar suffered at the hands of Amnon in 2 Samuel 13:14-17.)

As for the man, he is not only receiving punishment but also being forced to take responsibility for his actions. Had he been executed or exiled, the woman would have been left alone and unable to marry. The prescription of the Law was not unfair. Rather, the wisdom of God's Law comes into focus.

Deuteronomy 24:1—Was divorce easy in Old Testament times?

Divorce has always been a tragic failure to live up to God's original plan for marriage (Genesis 2:24). Jesus, commenting on this passage, remarked that Moses permitted divorce due to the hardness of people's hearts (Matthew 19:8). Some rabbis permitted divorce for any reason, others only for adultery. Most people weren't trying hard enough to make their marriages work. The provision of a certificate of divorce may seem like a callous dismissal of the woman's rights and feelings, but actually, it's just the opposite. It protected the woman from future claims by her former husband, thus improving her chances of remarriage.

Deuteronomy 34:1-12—How did Moses record his own death?

He didn't. All five books of the Law were attributed to Moses, for he was likely the human impetus behind them. But we need not believe Moses wrote every chapter, just as we need not believe Solomon wrote every proverb or David wrote every psalm.

6

Joshua to Esther

Joshua 2:1—Was Rahab a prostitute or an innkeeper?

This common word (*zonah*) means "prostitute" and occurs nearly 100 times in the Old Testament. In later Judaism the scandal of a prostitute serving as a model of faith led some to opine that Rahab was only an innkeeper. Yet some ancient inns reputedly served brothels, so Rahab could have been both prostitute and innkeeper. Today some prefer the "innkeeper" option, scandalized that God would choose a prostitute to work through or to save, especially because her name crops up in Jesus' ancestry (Matthew 1:5). But her reputation is a joyous reminder that we are never beyond redemption.

Joshua 2:4-6—Did Rahab sin by lying?

Rahab ranks with the great women of faith, and she is commended in Hebrews 11:31. She sided with the people of God and did her best to support them. She is not commended for lying per se. The book of Joshua reports what happened as it happened. It does not always offer a value judgment on what is happening. Sometimes we act inconsistently with the moral will of God yet are blessed anyway. Rahab is not praised for lying, but for her faith, by which she saved herself and her family as well.

Joshua 6:20-21—When did Israel attack Jericho? And why—couldn't the people have been given the chance to turn to God?

There are two major proposals for the dating of the conquest under Joshua: the late fifteenth century BC (approximately 1406) and the early thirteenth century BC (1290 is one suggestion). The evidence can be made to support either date, though I think the thirteenth century fits better. Jericho was a major urban center and a strategic military target for the invading Israelites, with a larger population than the second city of the region, Ai, which had a total of 12,000 adult inhabitants (Joshua 8:25).

These Canaanites did have a chance to repent. God was patient for generations (Genesis 15:16; Number 14:18; Psalm 103:8). And though murder was forbidden under the old covenant, judicial killing was not. This constitutes a major difference between the Testaments. In the Old Testament, the religious community was also a political entity. In the New Testament and under the new covenant, church and state are separate. To put it another way, under the first covenant, whatever the people of God did, the government was doing. These days, Christians have no authority to collect taxes, wage war, apportion land, and the like. Through Israel the Lord was punishing the Canaanites—and certainly not because of the Israelites' own virtue (Deuteronomy 9:4-6).

Joshua 10:12-14—Did NASA find the missing day?

This is a popular hoax. Regardless of how one interprets Joshua 10 (as poetic license, as a dilation of space-time, or as an astronomic miracle), there is no empirical proof for the elongated (or missing) day. Those who are committed to the Bible and to truth honor God by checking their facts, not by spreading rumors.

Joshua 21:43—Does archaeology support the account of Israel's conquest of Canaan?

Yes, but Joshua records the destruction of only three cities: Jericho (6:24), Ai (8:19,28), and Hazor (11:11). This means that we should expect more evidence of displacement than of destruction, at least in the remaining cities. And the fact that the archaeological evidence is not abundant should not be a problem for us. The archaeological evidence for the Norman conquest of England (AD 1066) is poorer than might be thought. This hardly means that the Norman French did not invade and assume power.

I was told in religion classes that Joshua described a blitzkrieg. Yet this is to misrepresent Joshua. Joshua 11:18 and 13:1 speak of a slow and arduous process, in keeping with the wisdom of God in Deuteronomy 7:22, where he explains that he will drive out the nations little by little. Eventually Israel received all the land the Lord had promised. The land promise (Genesis 12:1,6-7) was initially fulfilled in the time of Joshua, and it was symbolically fulfilled in the return from exile and the reign of the Messiah (Jeremiah 23:8).

Judges 4:4—Some churches teach that women should not speak publicly, so when Deborah led Israel, was she sinning?

Many conservative churches save the top leadership positions for males, though often with mixed feelings. After all, Paul, the same apostle who forbids women to preach to men (1 Timothy 2:11-12), assumes they will pray and prophesy publicly (1 Corinthians 11:5). And many of Paul's associates in ministry were women. The church is not a nation, so Deborah's example does not apply directly to our situation today. And she was certainly not sinning.

Judges 11:30-39—Did Jephthah sacrifice his daughter as a burnt offering, or did he simply sacrifice her right to marry?

Jephthah made a stunningly rash vow—and kept it. The Hebrew word for the sacrifice (11:31) always means a burnt offering (the Greek

Old Testament has *holocaust*), so a simple reading seems to indicate that he sacrificed his daughter's life (though not all interpreters agree). A similar example likely to produce shock in readers is Judges 1:6, where victors sliced off their enemies' thumbs and big toes. Chapter 19 is as graphic as it is barbaric, describing gang rape, mutilation, and callousness toward defenseless women.

But recording an event is not the same as approving it. Then as now, when everyone does what he sees fit (17:6; 21:25), atrocities happen. People need a leader—especially a divine one. Only in the Messiah would the true sovereign take the throne: the God-man, Jesus Christ.

Judges 14:1-4—How could Samson's marriage to a Philistine be from the Lord?

The Scriptures do not permit deliberate marriage outside the faith. (See entry for Ezra 10:11.) Samson's action was consistent with his lack of personal and spiritual maturity. It is not commended; it is only related. The text tells us that in his providence, the Lord used Samson's poor decision to give Israel an advantage in their struggle against their enemies, the Philistines. Numbers 20:8-12 provides a somewhat similar situation. Moses disobeys God, striking the rock instead of speaking to it, yet God blesses the people with water all the same.

We must be careful about how we discern the Lord's will. His sovereign purposes override our own. Even the cross was "from the Lord." What humans did was wrong, yet God used their actions for his purposes (Acts 2:23).

Judges 16:28-30—Was Samson a suicide terrorist?

Samson's final feat was a supernatural event, so he is not a strict parallel to the suicide bombers we see today. Samson was immature and vindictive (Judges 15:3,11), killing 3000 Philistines in revenge for having lost his eyes. This is not an example for us to emulate. Violence was permitted under the old covenant, but Jesus commands his followers to love their enemies.

Ruth 3:1-14—When Ruth sneaks up on Boaz and sleeps next to him, is she being immodest or even immoral?

Ruth was not asking Boaz to do anything immoral, but to marry her (verse 9). The corner of his garment implies the protection of marriage (Ezekiel 16:8). Next, when she lay at his feet (verse 14), no one saw, so no one was scandalized. Ruth had a noble character (verse 11), and in this matter she approached her prospective husband honorably.

1 Samuel 4:18—Is this passage a warning against obesity?

Not really. Eli had literally fattened himself from the offerings of the people (2:29), just as his wicked sons fattened themselves in violation of kosher law (2:12-17). Eglon was another fat man of the Bible (Judges 3:17-22), though we find no condemnation of his great girth. The Bible does not describe an ideal body shape. Moreover, what is appealing in one generation or culture may well be appalling in another. Dieting is a modern obsession, peculiar to the rich and the well-fed (Amos 4:1; James 5:5).

However, our body weight does relate to an important biblical principle—stewardship. If our bodies are temples of the Holy Spirit (1 Corinthians 6:19), we ought to take care of them with reverence.

1 Samuel 17:4—How could Goliath be nine feet tall?

The most notorious giant in the Bible, "a champion named Goliath," stood nine feet four (284 centimeters). A lesser-known giant in Old Testament times was Og, King of Bashan, whose iron bed was thirteen feet long—not that this length was his height. Gigantism in our day has produced individuals nearing the nine-foot mark, so we don't need to cast aspersions on the truthfulness of the Scriptures. If five feet four was the average male height, Goliath impressively towered more than four feet above the other warriors. (If his height was measured by the "short cubit," three inches shorter than the standard cubit, he would be seven feet ten. See "How long is a cubit?" on page 77.)

1 Samuel 19:9—How could God send an evil spirit?

In the Old Testament, secondary causes are often described as though they were primary causes (for examples, see Deuteronomy 8:3; Ezekiel 14:9; 20:25-26). Everything happens because God either wills it directly (he causes it, as in verse 21-23 of this chapter) or he wills indirectly (he allows it to take place, as in Isaiah 63:17), so nothing happens apart from the will of God.

The ancient Hebrews often described events of the second category as though they belonged to the first. In this way, they attributed everything to God. The trick is to figure out whether he directly caused something or merely allowed it (as in this passage). God sends evil spirits without any compromise of his purity (Habakkuk 1:13) only if the spirits do not emanate from God directly. I know this is not the way we moderns think of secondary causes, but this way of talking about events is common in the Bible (see also Judges 9:23; 1 Samuel 18:10; Isaiah 45:7; Ezekiel 29:13; Zechariah 11:16). As for temptation, it doesn't come from God (James 1:13), but from Satan (Matthew 4:3; 1 Timothy 3:7). The Lord indirectly uses Satan's work to test us.

1 Samuel 19:23-24—When the Spirit falls on Saul and he prophesies, is he saved?

Not at all. The Spirit falls on many people in both Testaments regardless of whether they are right with the Lord. See the comments on Numbers 11:25.

1 Samuel 19:24—Were people sometimes naked in the Bible?

In this and other passages (such as Isaiah 20:23; John 21:7), the people were simply not wearing their outer garments.

1 Samuel 28:3-17—Did Samuel really appear from the dead?

Apparently, the witch of Endor actually called up Samuel from the dead. The medium herself was shocked; whatever normally happened, this was no conjuring trick. The denizens of Sheol, the abode of the dead (*Hades* in the Greek Bible) are conscious and may be contacted, though they prefer not to be disturbed. Many Bible passages forbid necromancy (Leviticus 20:27; Deuteronomy 18:10-11; 1 Chronicles 10:13; Isaiah 8:19; 19:3; Galatians 5:20). We are forbidden to cross the barrier between life and death.

As for ghosts, though they have been feared in all cultures (see Matthew 14:26), the Bible gives no direct evidence that the disembodied spirits of humans haunt houses or terrorize the living. The Bible affirms the spiritual world but not the popular belief in ghosts.

2 Samuel 1:1-16—Why are there two accounts of Saul's death (1 Chronicles 10:1-5)? And is this a precedent for euthanasia?

The account of 1 Chronicles 10 mirrors the account of 1 Samuel 31, the chapter immediately preceding 2 Samuel 1. In the narrative, Saul takes his own life, whereas the Amalekite claims to have killed Saul himself (an "assisted suicide"?). For his audacity, the Amalekite loses his life. But was he telling the truth or simply hoping for some reward or bounty? The Bible twice relates that Saul fell on his own sword (his armor-bearer did the same). In the absence of corroborating testimony for the Amalekite's version of what happened, I conclude that he was lying. David judges the Amalekite by his own words.

As for how the Lord judges those who despair of life and take matters into their own hands, we must leave that to him.

2 Samuel 1:26—Were David and Jonathan lovers?

Jonathan was emotionally and spiritually close to David and encouraged him to find strength in God (1 Samuel 23:16). He protected David by informing him of Saul's stormy and volatile moods. What they shared—and this was wonderful—was camaraderie and genuine love, something David could never share with Saul, whose spirituality and will were weak. David had his own sexual struggles, but they were heterosexual (2 Samuel 11). As for Jonathan, 1 Samuel 18:3 relates that he loved David as he loved himself. He was living in accordance with God's Law (Leviticus 19:18—the second greatest commandment, according to Jesus), not perverting it.

2 Samuel 5:7—What is Zion?

The name *Zion* became attached to the city of David. It was the name of the hill on which the old Jebusite city had been built. After David's men captured it, *Zion* became synonymous with *Jerusalem.* Eventually Zion came to represent God's kingdom (Hebrews 12:22).

2 Samuel 7:11-16—Does this passage refer to Solomon or the Messiah?

The passage in its immediate context speaks of Solomon, but in its remote context, it points to the future messianic king. Notice that the Lord promises that the line of David would endure. How is this true if there is no Davidic descendant on the throne today? Actually, there is—Jesus reigns! He is wiser than Solomon and purer in heart than David, and he fulfills all the messianic prophecies of the Old Testament. God's love was never taken away from Solomon insofar as his blessing continues to remain on his descendant (Jesus Christ). Interestingly, by the time Jesus was born, the rabbis had already assigned this passage a messianic interpretation and connected it with Psalm 2.

So the text refers to both Solomon and Jesus. Does it imply that Solomon was saved? We cannot be dogmatic. The passage implies it as a possibility, but God is the judge of that.

2 Samuel 12:22-23—When are children accountable for their sin?

Regarding little ones who die, the Bible seems to teach the comforting message that we will see them again. Assuming David is correct in saying he would see his son again, we can be assured that those of us who have lost young children will be reunited with them.

The Bible does not say at which exact point a child becomes spiritually lost, though every inclination of his heart is evil from childhood

(Genesis 8:21). Inclinations are different from actual sins, or guilt. Children willfully sin long before they are able to make a mature decision regarding the gospel. The real question is how God views them: Are they accountable or not? After all, as Jesus said, the kingdom of heaven belongs to children.

We must not insist that those who never had the ability to process the gospel are lost. That would presumably apply to those born with mental disabilities. But it's a moot point. We can do only so much; the rest must be left in God's hands.

2 Samuel 23:24-39—How many mighty men were there, 30 or 37?

This group kept growing. The ultimate size was 53 according to 1 Chronicles 11:26-47, which was written later.

1 Kings 6:1—Are the 480 years in 1 Kings 6 to be taken literally?

If so, the Exodus took place about 1446 BC, because temple construction began in 966. But the number seems suspiciously symbolic (480 = 12 x 40, the number of God's covenant people multiplied by the number of years in one generation). If it is symbolic, the Exodus could easily have happened in the thirteenth century, and that is better in keeping with the archaeological evidence in Canaan.

1 Kings 7:23—If the Sea (or basin) was a circle with a 10-cubit diameter, the circumference was about 31.4 cubits, not 30 cubits. Did the Bible get it wrong?

The aim of the writer was to point out the impressive girth of this bronze structure, not to describe it as a geometer would. Some have suggested that 30 cubits was the internal diameter (excluding the thickness of the basin), yet it is more likely the biblical writer is giving us round numbers.

1 Kings 11:1-11—If Solomon broke all the rules in Deuteronomy 17, why was he considered to be such a wise king?

Solomon's wisdom was more prolific and renowned in his earlier years. In 1 Kings 11 we read that in his old age, his wives, whom he had married for political reasons, turned his heart to their gods. Solomon was careless; he compromised. Deuteronomy 17:18-20 is full of warnings so applicable to David's son that they seem to be tailor-made for him. Keep in mind that a monarchy was God's plan B. Plan A was a theocracy—the Lord alone was to occupy the throne (1 Samuel 8:7).

1 Kings 12–2 Chronicles 36—What is happening with the two kingdoms in Kings and Chronicles?

Following the two kingdoms requires patience and some historical background. The account alternates between the histories of Judah (the southern kingdom) and Israel (the northern kingdom). After Solomon's death, his son Rehoboam became king, but Jeroboam set up a rival kingdom complete with alternate sanctuaries, a priesthood, golden calves, and a blend of pagan religion and Judaism. The northern kingdom retained the name Israel, though it rebelled against Jerusalem and the house of David. The Lord punished Israel with Assyrian captivity in the late eighth century BC. The southern kingdom was more righteous and survived until the Babylonian captivity in the early sixth century BC. The Bible covers the histories of both kingdoms simultaneously in 1 and 2 Kings. Each has 20 kings (after Saul, David, and Solomon), so reading the account is like flipping between two television channels.

1 Kings 13:16-24—If the man of God was deceived, wasn't his punishment overly severe?

The young prophet disobeyed the word of the Lord. No one has the right to contravene the commands of God (Galatians 1:6-9). Sincerity was not the issue then, nor is it the issue now. Even sincere religious persons may be lost unless they are doing God's will (Matthew 7:21-23). The old prophet was from Bethel, a major site of idolatry among the northern Israelites. God allowed the young prophet to be tested, and unfortunately, he failed. A sobering lesson for all.

2 Kings 17–25—What happened to the lost tribes?

The Scriptures teach that the southern kingdom, Judah (which included the tribes of Judah, Benjamin, and Levi) remained somewhat true to the Lord for many years while the tribes in the northern kingdom, Israel, strayed. Contrary to what some groups teach, the lost tribes were not lost to the New World or to the western limit of the Old World. They were lost through intermarriage in the eighth century BC (2 Kings 17).

2 Kings 20:5-6—Are we faithless for going to doctors rather than seeking divine healing?

God is the Great Physician, and he heals not only supernaturally but also by natural means. Hezekiah was saved, but his healing included a medical component (verse 7). Trusting only in medicine (2 Chronicles 16:12) or technology is misguided, but so is rejecting the practical help made possible by virtue of the God-created world in which we live, including the healing properties of the body.

1 Chronicles 2:7—Should *Achar* be *Achan* (Joshua 7:1)?

The man's name could be either. The last letter of his name was either *resh* (*r*) or *nun* (*n*). In form these Hebrew letters are nearly identical and were sometimes confused. This is a good example of the triviality of common scribal errors.

1 Chronicles 4:10—Should we pray the prayer of Jabez?

The little prayer of 1 Chronicles 4 has sometimes been interpreted to mean that God wants to protect believers from suffering. Yet this belief is questionable. First, the translation is uncertain. Whereas the NIV has "keep me from harm so that I will be free from pain," the NKJV has "keep me from evil, that I may not *cause* pain." Second, what warrant do we have to assume the Lord will grant the same request on our lips? Suffering is part and parcel of the Christian life (Luke 9:23; 2 Timothy 3:12; 1 Peter 2:21). Third, popular Christian culture is obsessed with prosperity—receiving God's blessings and avoiding suffering. Jesus does offer comfort in our suffering, but a Christian walk without pain is as unrealistic as Christianity without a cross.

1 Chronicles 20:1—Why is David's adulterous affair with Bathsheba recounted in 2 Samuel 11:1-27 but not in 1 Chronicles 20?

The Chronicler omits the story of David's affair, but he does not whitewash the king. In fact, some parts of 1 Chronicles make David look worse than 2 Samuel does. For example, Satan (not God) incites him to take a census (21:1). David is forbidden to build the temple because he has shed so much blood (22:8; 28:3). These are simply differences in emphasis, much as the four Gospels emphasize different aspects of the life of Christ. God's word does not dress up our sins, secrets, and motives; it brings them into the light. Further reminders of David's disastrous affair are included in 1 Kings 15:5 and Psalm 51.

1 Chronicles 21:1—Who incited David to take the census, Satan or God (2 Samuel 24:1)?

In the census, God (2 Samuel 24) and Satan (1 Chronicles 21) work in the same event. Similarly concurrent action occurs in the crucifixion. According to Acts 2, although Satan seemed to have the upper hand, in fact Jesus was crucified by the will of God. God and Satan were involved in the same event. This dynamic also occurs in Job 1.

This explanation may not satisfy until we appreciate one further fact. The Old Testament often attributes sickness, death, and (in this case) sin directly to the Lord even though he only indirectly causes them. Everything is either done by God or permitted by God. (See comments on 1 Samuel 19:9.) So who caused David to order the census, God or Satan? The answer is both.

David's stubborn tendency to rely on statistics instead of relying on God to build and preserve the kingdom was deeply unspiritual. Even David's commander-in-chief, Joab—hardly a paragon of spirituality—finds the orders repugnant. Israel pays a heavy price—a plague (1 Chronicles 21:14) reduces the numbers of Israel, presumably in part because the census tax was not paid (see Exodus 30:12).

2 Chronicles 3:1—Is this Moriah the same place where Abraham nearly sacrificed Isaac?

There is no archaeological evidence, but the textual evidence is clear. The temple was built on the same mount where Abraham prepared his sacrifice (Genesis 22:2). Christ would later be crucified on Golgotha, another hill in the same immediate area.

2 Chronicles 34:14—What is the lost Book of the Law?

Josiah's reforms (621 BC) received their impetus from the discovery of the Torah, which had long been neglected. The long-lost book may well have been Deuteronomy itself.

2 Chronicles 36:22-23—Why would the Persian king finance the rebuilding of the temple?

As amazing as 2 Chronicles 36 and Ezra 1 sound, it is the truth. The Cyrus Cylinder, discovered in 1879, contains an edict recording imperial support for the religions of the peoples subjugated by the Persians. This was a reversal of the policy of the Assyrians and Babylonians, who aimed to crush the spirits of the conquered, not to strengthen their religions. The Persians strategically preferred to work through the existing governmental and religious infrastructure instead of demolishing it. The Cylinder is on display in London's British Museum.

Ezra 2—Why don't the numbers in Ezra 2 and Nehemiah 7 match more precisely? What does this say about the inspiration of the Bible?

The totals in the original manuscripts were probably correct. But even if they weren't, such discrepancies don't undermine the inspiration of the Bible unless we commit ourselves to the position that minor errors discredit the message. The Bible is inerrant in all the doctrines it affirms, and no biblical doctrine is affected by the exact totals of returning exiles. See "What do we mean when we say the Bible is inspired?" on pages 13-14.

Ezra 4:6—How does the chronology in Ezra 4 work?

The books of Ezra and Nehemiah have occasioned a good deal of chronological confusion. The first five verses of chapter 4 are set around the year 520. Zerubbabel is mentioned. Verses 6-23 constitute a long parenthesis. Verse 24 refers back to verse 5.

Haggai and Zechariah are mentioned in 5:1. They minister and prophesy from around 520 BC until the temple was rebuilt in 516 or 515 BC.

Like modern cinemas, biblical narratives often feature flashbacks and then fast-forward. The original readers and hearers of the books of Ezra and Nehemiah were probably familiar with the story and the history and were able to maintain focus. To us, however, millennia removed from the events, the historical parentheses are confusing. (Welcome to the club.)

Ezra 10:11—Why did Ezra force the Israelites to divorce their foreign wives?

Marriage outside the faith was expressly against the covenant (Exodus 34:15-16; Deuteronomy 7:3), though some provision was made for marrying outsiders (Deuteronomy 21:10-14). The same principle holds true under the new covenant (1 Corinthians 7:39; 2 Corinthians 6:14), though divorce from a unbelieving spouse is not mandated (1 Corinthians 7:12). See comments on 1 Corinthians 7:14. Be sure also to read Nehemiah 13:23-27.

Nehemiah 8:8—Were Ezra's assistants clarifying what he was teaching, or were they translating?

They could have been doing either or both. Many of the Jews in the Persian period no longer understood Hebrew. God often works through others to clarify his word in our lives (as in Acts 8:26-40). Then as now, when we understand the word, joy is the natural result (Nehemiah 8:12).

Nehemiah 11—Why are only Judah, Benjamin, and Levi mentioned? Where are the other tribes?

By the time of the Persian period, they had been deported or absorbed into the surrounding peoples. Jerusalem was the capital of the Judean kingdom (though sited in Benjamin), which remained somewhat more faithful to Yahweh than did the northern kingdom. As for the northern ten tribes, their blood was blended with that of foreigners, causing them to become lost (2 Kings 17).

Esther—Is Esther's canonicity suspect because it doesn't mention God and because it wasn't in the Dead Sea Scrolls?

Although the book of Esther does not include the word *God*, his presence is implicit in the fabric of the narrative. He protects his people through the courage of Esther and Mordecai, he causes the sleepless king to call for the archived record of Mordecai's service to the Persian Empire, and he works justice for Haman and the Jewish people alike. Those with eyes of faith recognize what is going on behind the scenes and see that the book is brimming over with God.

As for the Dead Sea Scrolls, no copies of Esther have yet been discovered—and this is unique among the Old Testament books. Yet part of this book may be among the hundreds of still-unidentified fragments.

Esther 2:16-17—Did Esther sin by entering the king's harem?

Strange as this feels to us, as soon as Esther was taken into the harem, she was legally his property, his concubine. Their sex would not have been illicit because it would not have been premarital. Her inclusion in his harem made the relationship marital.

The Old Testament records many customs that are odd to us (including slavery and polygamy), but that does not imply that they accurately reflected God's will. It only attests to the honesty and practicality of the biblical record.

7

Job to Malachi

Job–Song of Songs—How should we read the poetry of the Bible? Obviously it's not to be taken literally.

All literary genres in the Bible convey divine truth, and the poetry deserves to be read with humility and sensitivity to its biblical themes. Yet major differences exist between poetry and prose. Much of the Bible is poetry—around 30 percent. Nearly all the verses from Job through Song of Songs are verse. And much of the Prophets is also poetic. Literalizing poetry is problematic because figures taken literally contradict the intended meaning of the author. For more on this, see "Are we to read the Bible literally or figuratively?" on page 24.

Sometimes a straightforward historical account is retold poetically. We read of the Exodus from Egypt in Exodus 14. The poetic version follows in Exodus 15 (the Song of Moses) and is far more dramatic and colorful. This is allowable and even expected in poetry. Similarly, Judges 5 (the Song of Deborah) retells the straight narrative of Judges 4. Some of the details do not match up. Why? Because they do not need to, for the rules of expression are more flexible in poetry. Poetic license does not discredit the writer; it enhances the message, making it more memorable, bringing out important meaning, and maximizing its impact.

If we read Psalm 50:10 woodenly, the Lord has title to only a thousand hills. One thousand, to the ancient mind, is an enormous number and might as well be the largest possible number. Psalm 58:3, if taken literally, has unbelievers lying before they are even born, just as Psalm 51:5 would have us all born sinners. The language is hyperbolic and emphasizes the sinfulness of the wicked. Ancient readers knew the difference, and we modern readers should too.

Job—How much of the advice from Job's friends should we believe?

All of Job is inspired, yet its characters don't always understand or speak the truth. Like the overly cynical Ecclesiastes, Job's function in the canon is to correct popular theology—a way of thinking that is as current in our day as it was in Job's time.

So even though this meaty book comes to us by the inspiration of God, the speakers aren't always telling the whole truth. Satan speaks, and Job's friends—Eliphaz, Bildad, and Zophar—spout off nonsense, God himself upbraiding them (42:7-8). Yet some of what they say is right, and the apostle Paul even quotes Eliphaz (Job 5:13; 1 Corinthians 3:19). All of this underscores the fact that care is needed when citing the book of Job. The entire work is a rebuttal of the popular notion that things always go well with the righteous. Consider the context and the speaker before you frame a quote and put it up on your wall.

Job 26:12-13—What was Rahab?

In Canaanite cosmogonies (creation myths), the great dragon (Rahab, or Tiamat) was slain and cut in two. The top half became the heavens or sky, and the bottom half became the earth. In the few places in Scripture where the dragon is mentioned, the image is "demythologized" and turned on its head in order to show the superiority of Yahweh (Job 9:13; 26:12; Psalm 74:13; 89:10; Isaiah 27:1; 51:9; Ezekiel 29:3; 32:2; Revelation 12:1-17). There is no fearsome, watery chaos to threaten us, no beast to frighten us; the Lord reigns supreme.

Note: When referring to the primeval monster, the Hebrew word for *Rahab* is spelled differently than it is when referring to the harlot of Jericho (Joshua 2).

Job 40:15-24—Was the behemoth a dinosaur?

This is doubtful. The Living Bible is nearly alone in rendering *behemoth* as *hippopotamus*, though this rendering is possible. I have never found *elephant* in any translation. The Hebrew word probably doesn't refer to an aquatic dinosaur. In most versions the word is (wisely) left untranslated.

Behemoth normally refers to any large animal, like cattle. Dinosaurs (like quasars, black holes, blue-green algae, and DNA) were unknown in biblical times, and it would be unwise to infer their presence from a poetic passage in Job. These omissions are insignificant. The Bible focuses on humans and our relationship with God, not on the million fascinating facts of science and history.

Job 41:1—What was Leviathan?

Probably a crocodile. This beast also appears in Job 3:8; Psalm 74:14; 104:26 (where the term may refer to the whale); and Isaiah 27:1 (speaking of the heathen nations). The description at the end of Job is especially poetic, with fire coming out of Leviathan's mouth. Some believers think this is speaking of dinosaurs or even fire-breathing dragons. That's the sort of thing that happens when we confuse literary genres. We should read poetry with an eye for the figurative and read narrative in its straightforward, literal sense.

Psalm 82:1,6—Are we gods?

Gods normally means "false gods," objects of idolatry (Genesis

31:19). But in Psalm 82, it specifies political rulers. Here the Lord expresses his indignation against them for failing to champion the cause of the poor. Despite their arrogance, they will die "like every other ruler." As Jesus said in John 10:34-35, "Is it not written in your Law, 'I have said you are gods'? If he called them 'gods,' to whom the word of God came..." These are those to whom the word of God came—human beings.

We are not God or gods. Accepting this truth has been mankind's perennial struggle since Eden. Our natural bent is toward personal autonomy, as though we were the center of the universe. I hope those who are influenced by New Age thinking will humbly receive the word and not just grab at straws to support erroneous theology.

Psalm 90:4—With God, is a day a thousand years?

Psalm 90 does not say 1000 years *are* a day, but that they're *like* a day. Moses (to whom this psalm is attributed) adds, "...or like a watch in the night" (four hours was a Jewish watch). Psalm 90 underscores the swiftness of time (from God's perspective), and 2 Peter 3 uses the same thought to emphasize its slowness (from our perspective). This is poetry, not celestial mechanics.

Psalm 119—What is an acrostic?

In this psalm, each line and stanza begins with successive letters of the Hebrew alphabet. There are 22 letters (consonants) in all. Every stanza has eight lines, all of which begin with the same letter. Thus the first eight lines begin with *aleph,* the next eight with *beth,* and so on. The Hebrew Bible includes other acrostics, such as the substantial one in Lamentations, which also plays with the number 22.

Psalm 137:9—How could God (and his inspired word) refer to smashing babies? Are we to wish ill on our enemies?

This passage does *not* reveal God's heart, at least not as you and I have experienced it. Psalms, a sort of prayer book, faithfully reflects the outpourings of hearts some 2500 to 3000 years ago. God allowed this troubling passage to remain in the Psalter. Why? Perhaps it is left to be an encouragement to us also to pour out our hearts, to share our true feelings, rather than to go through the motions and pray or say the "right" things.

Honesty is commendable—the honesty of this psalmist (waiting out the Babylonian exile and bitterly struggling with his faith) and yours as well. Even though we may say shocking things to God, we can be assured that he listens. He doesn't tune us out when we are open with him. Candor needs to join faith and persistence if we are to pray as genuinely as the psalmist.

Psalms that invoke curses on an enemy, such as Psalms 35, 109, and 137, are called *imprecatory* psalms. Jesus taught, however, that we are not to curse our enemies. We are to bless them, pray for them, and even love them (Matthew 5:43-48). The old way must die because the new way of the Spirit has taken its place.

Proverbs 1:1—Did Solomon write Proverbs?

Yes and no. The entire collection was attributed to him, yet he is only one of the many contributors. Chapters 1–9 are of unknown origin, and 22:17–24:14 are "The Sayings of the Wise." Chapter 30 is from Agur, and 31:1-9 is from King Lemuel. The only part overtly assigned to Solomon authorship is 10:1–22:16, a total of around 350 proverbs. Yet 1 Kings 4:32 tells us that the great king spoke 3000 proverbs. This means 88 percent of his pithy sayings did not survive!

Proverbs 16:3—Why is this promise not always fulfilled?

A single biblical passage may not contain the comprehensive truth on a subject, and this principle definitely applies to Proverbs. Most of the proverbs are life generalizations; they do not tell us everything we might like to know. Commit your plans to the Lord, and they will succeed—that is, involve God. And yet the verse must be read in the light of other biblical passages that encourage us to take God's will into account.

Proverbs 22:6 is another generalization, not an ironclad promise. It highlights the correlation between godly instruction and how our children turn out. Some excellent parents have rebellious children, just as some children grow up to be outstanding persons despite atrocious parenting. Proverbs 28:19 is another example. Not everyone who works hard succeeds, though there is a correlation. When we don't succeed, sin or halfheartedness may be at fault—but not necessarily. Faith is not mechanical. We do not always get our way just because we have asked nicely and added, "In Jesus' name."

Proverbs 29:18—Is this verse talking about having a vision for our lives?

The King James Version rendering makes it sound that way. Yet *vision* there is a prophetic revelation (Numbers 12:6); the verse is not about having vision for your life. When there is no word from God, people go astray and mess up their lives (see 1 Samuel 3:1,7.) The KJV rendering has been improved in the ESV ("prophetic vision") and better yet in the NIV ("revelation").

Proverbs 29:15—Does this verse call for spanking?

Jesus never spoke against the practice. Of course, abuse—physical, verbal, sexual, whatever—seriously messes up kids. Yet age-appropriate spanking does not necessarily have negative effects when administered in an atmosphere of love and acceptance. For some children (such as some children with mental health challenges), spanking does not work and may cause psychological damage, even when administered in love. Yet behavior modification and reinforcement is an essential part of parenting, along with nurture.

For a biblical perspective, explore the Old Testament. Proverbs 29 has several pretty clear passages (verses 15,17,19,21). Hebrews 12 and many other passages also speak to this. Read some Christian parenting books, and if you are a father, I sincerely hope you will follow the word of God as you train your children and lead your family spiritually.

Proverbs 31:4-7—Do these verses teach us anything about medical marijuana use?

The advice of a physician is usually the better part of wisdom. Self-medication is not. Proverbs 31 is the classic text for analgesics of various kinds. Yet we should hesitate to encourage medication if there is another route to wholeness, such as prayer, discussion, exercise, diet, and worship. The normal caveats about use of any strong substance apply: escapism, effects on others, addiction, funding crime. And all the balancing truths of the Bible must be taken into account, including these:

- Much of Jesus' ministry included alleviating pain and suffering. Nothing is inherently wrong with medication.

- Character formation should be emphasized, not its deferment, which easily happens when drug dependence is fostered.

- Some sins do not obviously hurt others, yet non-harm isn't the sole criterion for morality. (Private vanity or profanity is still unrighteous.)

- Human legislation does not make sin permissible. Human laws seldom call us to the standard of God's word. (Laws regulate divorce, prostitution, and pornography, yet that doesn't exempt us from God's call to holiness.)

Ecclesiastes—Why is this book so negative?

Life becomes a burden when we live for ourselves and not for God (2:17; 6:3; 7:1). Ecclesiastes shows us how empty life can be when we live for the things of this world and not for God. In some ways Ecclesiastes approaches theology from the reverse angle of Job. In Job, conventional wisdom has the Lord micromanaging the universe, excessively involved in the world. Rewards and punishments are dispensed in real time. In Ecclesiastes this view is challenged, so much so that the Lord feels distant, uninvolved in the world. Religion has nearly become philosophy. Yet at least Solomon's conclusion (12:13-14) is balanced.

Ecclesiastes 3:8—Is there really a time to hate?

An ethic of hatred was condoned and even inculcated in Old Testament times. Jesus Christ taught otherwise (Matthew 5:44). We are called to rise above the level of the world (Romans 12:17-21) and not to hate. Jesus changed the rules.

Ecclesiastes 3:21—Do animals go to heaven?

When our German shepherd died in 1970, I cried all day. I would have done anything to see her again or to believe I would see her again. Wishful thinking can find anything in a verse of Scripture, but the Bible simply doesn't provide a definitive answer to this question.

Song of Solomon—Is this an allegory of Christ's love for us, or is it really about sexual love?

This is not the only racy section of Scripture, but it does stand out. Contrary to the puritanical tendencies of much of religion, the Bible does not conceal the truth about "the birds and the bees." Sexuality and marriage make their appearance in the first couple of pages of Scripture. This is no mere allegory. On the other hand, the apostle Paul compares Christ's relationship with the church to a marriage (Ephesians 5), so many theologians have understandably seen in Song of Solomon a beautiful picture of Christ and his bride, the church.

Isaiah—Malachi—How did the prophets get their messages from God?

The answer surprises most people. The prophets often received their prophetic messages in visions, normally as they slept. Check 1 Chronicles 17:3; Isaiah 21:2; Jeremiah 31:26; Lamentations 2:9; Hosea 12:10; Joel 2:28; Micah 3:6; Zechariah 4:1; and Acts 2:17-18. Moses was a conspicuous exception to this general rule (Numbers 12:6-8).

Isaiah 6:2—Do angels have wings?

Seraphs and cherubs are guardian spirits. Other angels normally appear as humans; in fact, they are most often indistinguishable from them. The Hebrew word *mala'k* and the Greek word *angelos* both mean either angel or messenger. Angels don't have wings, despite the suggestive description of the archangel Gabriel as being in "swift flight" (Daniel 9:21).

Isaiah 7:14—Does this refer to a virgin or simply a young woman?

The Hebrew *'almah* means a young woman, though unless she was married this would have been understood as a virgin. The Jewish translators of the Bible into Greek rendered *'almah* as *parthenos* (virgin). The notion of a virgin birth precedes Christianity.

Isaiah 8:16—Who wrote Isaiah and when?

Bisecting Isaiah after chapter 39 simply because of explicit prophecies about Cyrus in chapters 44 and 45 is unacceptable. Analysis should rest on sound literary and theological grounds, not on prejudice against prophecy. What is the biblical evidence? Isaiah 8:16 indicates Isaiah had his disciples write down his prophecies, so we know the book has been edited. Several biblical books have multiple authorship (including Joshua, Psalms, and 1 Corinthians), and the Bible itself is a multiauthor collection. Regardless of when Isaiah 40–66 was written, it is a vehicle for the message of God and includes many words of encouragement and admonition.

Isaiah 14:12—Does this refer to Satan? Where did the name Lucifer come from? And when did Satan fall?

The word *Lucifer* occurs in the Latin Vulgate translation (written in about AD 400) in three locations, two of which refer to dawn and the third to the King of Babylon (Isaiah 14:12). In the King James Version, the word *Lucifer* appears only in this passage. In Latin it means "light bearer." Because *Lucifer* occurs in no original Hebrew or Aramaic Old Testament manuscript, the modern versions dropped it.

The word *Satan*, which appears in both New and Old Testaments, has been retained wherever it is found. The king of Babylon, however—whose fall resembles that of Satan, even though that is not the immediate subject of Isaiah 14—is rightly called "morning star" (NIV) or "day star" (RSV). The Bible does not say when Satan fell, though presumably this took place before the creation of mankind.

Isaiah 34:14—What is Lilith?

This word is found only in this passage. It comes from the Hebrew word for night (*laylah*). It is rendered variously as "night creatures" (NIV), "night monster" (NASB), "Lilith" (NRSV and Darby), *onokentauros* or donkey-centaur (LXX), *le spectre de la nuit* (French Louis Segond), *Lilit* (Italian Nuova Riveduta), *Kobold* (Luther), and *Lamia* or witch (Latin Vulgate and Spanish Reina Valera). Many translators did not know what to do with this unusual word. A medieval legend names Lilith as a disobedient wife of Adam. Since we are dealing with legend, and since the passage in which the word in question is found is both poetic and apocalyptic, we cannot draw any conclusions about the mysterious "night hag."

Isaiah 40:22—Is this an early indication that the earth is round?

The verse does portray the earth as round, yet what does "round" mean? The text reads, "He sits enthroned above the circle of the earth, and its people are like grasshoppers. He stretches out the heavens like a canopy, and spreads them out like a tent to live in."

The earth is poetically described as a circle. A circle is two-dimensional, and unless rotated about an axis, it is "stretched out" like a canopy. Many of the ancients conceived of the earth as a disk covered by a hemispherical vault. This passage reflects that understanding and should not be pressed to yield scientific insight into the shape of our planet. (Nor does "stretch" refer to the expansion of space following the Big Bang.)

This passage and others like it were never intended to comment on the dimensions or shape of the earth, any more than the Bible's use of *sunrise* and *sunset* was meant to impart the old Ptolemaic geocentric dogma. Poetry paints a picture, and if the elements are wrested from their literary context, the picture is distorted.

Isaiah 45:7—Did God create evil?

We know that God is good. Evil was not created, just as good was not created. Evil is the effect of free moral agents resisting God's will; it doesn't exist apart from that. Consider this illustration: Heat is a real thing, but cold is not; it is only the absence of heat. Our universe is not somehow dualistic, with two opposite forces—good and evil—keeping one another in some sort of cosmic check.

It is fair to ask, why did God create *this* universe? Couldn't he have made a world without evil, a world where everyone would choose to do good, to follow him? The answer is that goodness is possible for us humans only when we have a choice. God could certainly have chosen not to create freewill creatures. Yet the benefit must have been worth the risk, better than the alternative of creating nothing. Here are more thoughts to ponder:

- Suffering is increased because we are in a fallen world into which sin has made a dramatic and often catastrophic entrance (Genesis 3:16-17). Suffering often affords an opportunity for God to be glorified (John 9:1-3).

- Abraham struggled with God's judgment of Sodom and Gomorrah (Genesis 18:25). Read the account carefully. The important point is not the percentage of the populace who survived. The issue is Abraham's faith in a just God as he exclaims, "Will not the Judge of all the earth do right?" A number of other biblical characters shared a similar concern (see Psalm 73; Jeremiah 12:1; Habakkuk 1:3).

- Children sometimes wander; they become wayward. Why

do we choose to have them in the first place, given the possibility that they might embrace a life of crime or even turn against us? Why not play it safe and not procreate? We go ahead because the reward (love) is worth the risk (Isaiah 29:24; Luke 15:13).

- Spiritual growth can take place through suffering even if we never receive the explanation for why it has come into our lives, as happened with Job. When we persevere through suffering, our character grows (Romans 5:3-4).

- God uses suffering to make us more like his Son so that we may be in relationship with him (Romans 8:28-29).

- One day, suffering will end (Revelation 21–22).

Christianity offers no comprehensive explanation for suffering, much less an escape from pain—otherwise people would be coming into the church in droves. Yet Christ does promise grace to endure and shows us that through the cross, God himself has fully shown his heart and his competence to intimately meet our need, even when we are in dark places.

To ask the question is therapeutic; to ignore it may be injurious to your faith. Part of maturing spiritually is being real enough to work through your concerns, even if they are only partly resolved. At the end of it all, God isn't the originator of evil, pain, and suffering. He is the source of all goodness, comfort, and relief.

Isaiah 47:13—Can horoscopes ever be useful?

Your fortune, astrologers say, is determined by the sign under which you were born. That is, luck depends on one's birth date. But individual existence precedes actual birth date. (How do the stars "know" whether you are still *in utero* or have already been delivered?) Moreover, distant objects have virtually no gravitational or magnetic effect on our bodies. The book you are holding in your hand has far more pull on you than any constellation in the heavens. The slight gravitational attraction between objects in the room where you're sitting and your body is millions of times more powerful than the force of Mars or Leo.

Horoscopes are impossibly general. The prediction for Scorpio could equally well apply to Pisces or Taurus. There is a simple reason for this: The more specific these pseudoscientific prophecies, the more often they are seen to be nonsensical. Those whose incomes are bound up in astrology are not likely to risk their own fortune by moving out of the realm of the vague.

The Bible portrays astrologers as inept for good reason (Daniel 2:10; 4:7; 5:7-8). Astrology is associated with idolatry, and as we have seen, it is not based on reason. Horoscopes are useful only for a good laugh. Marry freely—any "sign" of the 12 will do. As long as a marriage is spiritually grounded, you will continue to grow closer. And that attractive force is worth more than gold.

Isaiah 64:6—Is *all* our righteousness like filthy rags?

No. Scripture rejects works-salvation and dead faith. The religious acts Isaiah describes in this verse are filthy not because humans always fail—though that is true—but because there is no real relationship with God (verse 7). Isaiah 1 paints a vivid picture of the apostasy of the people of God. This is the reason why they are clad in filthy rags; it's not because their best isn't good enough. In contrast, Scripture uses clean garments to represent a life devoted to the Lord (Zechariah 3:3-5; Revelation 3:4,18; 19:14). In short, when we stop sinning, we are clean in God's eyes (Isaiah 1:16). Isaiah 64:6 should never be used as an excuse not to give our best to the Lord.

Isaiah 65:17—Why would God create new heavens and earth if people will only be able to go to heaven or hell?

Isaiah 65:17 and 66:22 describe the future, glorious state of Israel as "a new heavens and a new earth." The prophet foretells an age of hope after the return from the exile (sixth century BC). One must appreciate the historical situation. If the description was not to be taken literally in Isaiah's time, neither would Peter necessarily have meant it literally when he picked up the theme in his second letter (2 Peter 3:13). Some groups force a literal interpretation on the passage. Yet the descriptions in the final chapters of Isaiah are highly metaphorical. They are best understood by treating them according to their literary genre, which is prophecy and poetry.

"The heavens and the earth" represent the entire cosmos, all that there is. A new heavens and earth suggest a fresh start, a new beginning. Presumably heaven does not need to be recreated. (God has always kept his abode pure.) Whether there will be a new planet Earth is a matter for debate, but in my opinion this is unlikely—even if nice to think about.

Jeremiah 8:8—What is the "lying pen" of the scribes?

I have often read Jeremiah 8 and wondered the same thing. The scribes copied the word of God faithfully (see Jeremiah 36:2,4,32), but they twisted the Scriptures to their own destruction, as Jeremiah laments (see also 2 Peter 3:16.) For a leader to misrepresent God is a serious thing.

Jeremiah 29:11-14—Does this promise apply to an individual's future?

This has become a favorite passage for many, perhaps because God's heart shines through, and we see his desire for our well-being. It also resonates with our individualistic spirit—especially when we read the passage out of context.

The prophet has just reminded the exiled people of God that their stay in Babylon will not be short. Exile was definitely not their plan A. This was plan B, and the undesirable experience was to last 70 years (25:11; 29:10). God promised relief, but as in the case of the Exodus, it would not come for a few generations.

God's plan for your life probably doesn't include health, wealth, and the dream job. It is to become conformed to the character of

Christ through a process of suffering and perseverance (Romans 5:1-3; 8:17,28-29; 12:1-2). Aim to be like Christ as much as you can, and you will discover his will.

Lamentations 2:14—Why does Jeremiah criticize the other prophets?

Jeremiah's opponents made up their own religion, minimized sin, and diluted the word of God, accommodating it to the world's standards (Jeremiah 5:13,30-31; 6:13-14; 23:9-40). The *false* prophets assured Judah their spiritual condition was not serious. Jeremiah's message was uncompromising, and he proclaimed it boldly for 40 years (626–586 BC) until Jerusalem fell to the Babylonians. The book of Jeremiah is the "before," Lamentations the "after." In biblical times as now, the true prophets were far outnumbered by the false ones (1 Kings 18:22; 22:6-23; Matthew 7:15-20; 2 Peter 1:2-3).

Lamentations 4:10—Were some Jewish people cannibals?

Cannibalism was practiced in some times of extreme hunger, as has been the case rarely throughout human history. Yet it should not be taken as characterizing the Jews.

The books of the Law warned that if the people ignored God's commands, their enemies would come, besiege their cities, and drive them into dark places, including otherwise unthinkable actions (Leviticus 26:29; Deuteronomy 28:53-57). Later the prophets warned the covenant people, reminding them of what would await them if they ignored the Law (Jeremiah 19:9; Ezekiel 5:10). Sadly, when God gave them over to their enemies, his people on occasion did practice cannibalism (2 Kings 6:28-29), notably during the Babylonian siege of Jerusalem (Lamentations 2:20; 4:10).

Ezekiel 1—Did Ezekiel see a UFO?

The vision of Ezekiel 1 is of God, not a UFO. Hundreds of extrasolar planets have been discovered, not to mention the planets and moons in our solar system, but to date we have no unequivocal evidence for life, even as small as a bacterium. What if something did turn up? Here's my response:

- This is awesome!

- Is this life advanced?

- If the creatures are advanced, are they moral beings?

- If they are moral, have they fallen?

- If they have fallen, the sacrifice of the one who is Lord of heaven and earth—and who fills heaven and earth—is more than ample to meet their need.

As for claims of sightings and abductions, we should be skeptical. Many centuries ago, folks believed in trolls, fairies, goblins, sprites, leprechauns, and all sorts of other mysterious creatures. Such claims these days are no longer fashionable and have largely disappeared. But belief in ET (extraterrestrials) has taken over. One in four Americans now believes our world has been visited by aliens.[7] It is part of the mythology of our age.

Ezekiel 18:20—Does this verse contradict Exodus 20:5? How is the sin of the parents visited on their children?

Exodus 20:5, highlighting God's uncompromising holiness, mentions the consequences of sin—in this case, idolatry—which often last three or four generations. The innocent suffer for the sin of the parents, just as the child of an alcoholic suffers for the father's sins through beatings, psychological damage, and so on. He isn't being directly punished for his own sin, yet the sins are being visited on him—having an impact on him—because he is part of the network of relationships that connect him with the source of sinful actions (in this case, the father). And yet in his goodness, God's blessing on the families of those who honor him may reach a thousand generations.

Ezekiel 18:20 pertains to a different subject, one's own personal responsibility. "The soul who sins is the one who will die." The sober reality is that although God is fair, neither arbitrary nor cruel, and desires all to be right with him (Ezekiel 18:32), he doesn't necessarily protect us from others. Their sin affects us, in some cases severely. Indirectly speaking, we share the punishment for their wrongdoing.

Ezekiel 37:2—Does this verse describe the way our bodies will be resurrected at the last day?

This chapter colorfully foretells the national "resurrection" that took place in the sixth century BC when the captives were permitted to return to Israel. Still, the passage is suggestive of the last resurrection, when all mankind will rise and give an accounting for their deeds.

Ezekiel 38:2—Who are Gog and Magog?

This is symbolism; God is reassuring the Jews that he will take care of them. There is no specific nation or event in mind; Gog and Magog symbolize any power that tries to harm Israel. They are not modern nations (Russia, China, North Korea) or persons (Stalin, Mao, Castro). Gog and Magog represent the enemies of God's people.

Ezekiel 40–48—Is this vision of a heavenly temple or one that will be built on earth?

Like the description of the New Jerusalem in Revelation 21, the passage combines literal and metaphorical elements. Both present a heavenly vision of an earthly reality and make more sense taken figuratively rather than literally. The stylized division of the land (Ezekiel 47–48) is geographically implausible. The Dead Sea turns to fresh water (47:8; see Zechariah 14:8). In other words, we should not expect the Jerusalem temple to be rebuilt. Atonement is made for the people through offerings (Ezekiel 45:17), something unthinkable after the completed work of the cross. Rather, the passage speaks of the messianic age already set in motion by the first coming of Christ.

Daniel 1:12-16—Why did God make us carnivores?

Genesis pictures a primordial vegetarianism, but this is not necessarily the Lord's will for us today. Mark 7:19, Hebrews 13:9, and Colossians 2:21 suggest the opposite.

Daniel avoided the ritually unclean (non-kosher) fare of the Babylonian court out of reverence for God. A man of principle, he was unwilling to compromise his obedience to Mosaic dietary restrictions. Though he ate only vegetables, at least for a while—I assume he still took part in the Passover meal and ingested flesh on other carnivorous occasions—he was healthier than whose who ate the rich food of the king.

Jesus himself caught and cooked fish (John 21). Diet is an area of freedom for Christians, and we must respect others' opinions. Mine is that, if our Lord wasn't a vegetarian, I do not need to be one either.

Daniel 4:29-33—What happened to Nebuchadnezzar?

Nebuchadnezzar was punished for his arrogance with the psychological disorder called boanthropy, the delusion that one is a bovine. (This is similar to lycanthropy, the belief that one is a wolf or even a werewolf.) Like the Babylonian king, we all have two sides—Jekyll and Hyde, the flesh and the spirit—as Paul makes clear in Romans 6–8 and Galatians 5. When we are not in our right mind, we do things we regret. And yet with God's Spirit, we accept his sovereignty in our lives and rise above our "animal" nature.

Daniel 5:25—What is the meaning of the writing on the wall?

It means the game is up. *Mene, tekel,* and *upharsin* are units of weight and money. They also mean "numbered," "weighed," and "divided." The days of the Babylonian king are numbered. He has been weighed, tried, and found wanting. As a result, his kingdom will be divided between the Persians and the Medes. In the same way, we will one day face the judge of all mankind, as deep down most persons suspect, know, fear, or hope (Acts 17:31).

Hosea–Malachi–What is the difference between the major prophets and minor prophets?

In Latin, the language of Western medieval scholarship and theology, *major* means "greater," and *minor* means "lesser." The terms have to do only with their length, not their theological importance. (Although admittedly the book of Isaiah, which the New Testament quotes more than any other prophetic book and is replete with references to the coming Messiah, is hardly on the same level of importance with, say, Obadiah.) The major prophets are the longer books (Isaiah–Ezekiel and usually Daniel); the minor prophets are the shorter books.

Hosea 1:2–Did Hosea really marry a prostitute?

Though the text makes most readers uncomfortable, softening it (as if Hosea married a prostitute only proleptically) reduces the full effect of Hosea's message of grace: God loved us when we were unclean sinners, not after we came clean. Adultery is a common biblical image for spiritual unfaithfulness (James 4:4).

Hosea 1:4–Why would God punish Jehu for following a divine command (2 Kings 9:7)?

Jehu was told to eradicate the house of Ahab, the spiritually crooked leaders of the kingdom of Israel. Yet he attacked also the kingdom of Judah, slaughtering many sympathetic to Ahab (and his Baal worship). Jehu may have meant well, but he apparently overstepped the bounds of his divine commission.

Joel 2:28-32–When are the last days? How will we know when it's time?

According to Peter on the day of Pentecost, quoting Joel 2, the last days are here (Acts 2:16-21). This means also that the various apocalyptic signs (darkened sun, bloody moon, and the like) are symbols. For similar usage of such stock symbols, see Isaiah 13; 30:26; 34. This suggests Peter referred to the last days of Israel as a national covenant community as well as the inauguration of the final phase of human history, often referred to in the New Testament.

Many passages in the prophets foretell the messianic age. Besides such theologically central chapters as Isaiah 53, Jeremiah 31, and Ezekiel 34, the minor prophets are heavily messianic. For example, Micah 5:1-5 speaks of the birth of the Messiah, 7:6 of the divisiveness of his ministry, and 7:15 of a renewal of miracles in his day. Zechariah is dripping with messianic material, prophesying Christ's ministry, death, kingship, and purification for our sins (2:10; 3:8; 9:9; 11:12; 12:10; 13:1,7; 14:9). Malachi speaks of the forerunner of the Messiah, John the Baptist (3:1-2; 4:5-6), during whose ministry God himself suddenly visits the earth. Nearly all the prophetic material was penned between the eighth and fifth centuries BC—long before its fulfillment in Jesus Christ, through whom the kingdom of God has begun to come to earth. The last days will end at the second coming of Christ.

Here's the short answer: The last days are now.

Amos 5:18-20—What is the day of the Lord?

It's not what the Jews were expecting. The people of Israel expected vindication, but rejection by Yahweh was certain because of their hypocrisy. Parallels may exist in Matthew 3:7-10; 7:21-23. Here is a sobering warning for us too. Longing for the day of the Lord is a good thing, provided we are ready for the judgment. Self-deception—if we are not living in faith (Luke 18:8; Revelation 3:14-22)—is not.

Amos 9:7—Before Christ, was God at work in all the nations?

Israel was the chosen people, and with that privilege came responsibility (Psalm 147:20; Amos 3:2). Yet God's concern for the other nations is abundantly evident in Scripture (Psalm 67:4; Jeremiah 12:17). So is the fact that he has worked in their history (Amos 9:7). The God of the Hebrews reigns not only in Israel; he is the Lord of the entire earth.

Amos 9:11-12—When will Israel be restored?

Amos 9:11-15 predicted the return of Israel from exile, which took place in the sixth century BC. But this passage also points to something bigger. According to James, presiding at the council of Jerusalem in AD 49, this passage was fulfilled in the Gentile mission (Acts 15:16-17). Gentiles and Jews are now joined together in the church as God raises up "David's fallen tent." For a parallel, see Joel 2:28–3:2 and Peter's interpretation in Acts 2:16-21. If this view is correct, Israel has already been restored. For more, see the entry on Romans 11:25-27.

Jonah 1:1,17—Was Jonah a real person? Was he really swallowed by a whale?

The Bible portrays Jonah as a real, historical figure. This eighth-century prophet is also mentioned in 2 Kings 14:25. As for the whale, the text refers to "a great fish," but zoological precision is not the aim. The point of this prophetic book, that God cares for the Gentiles (even when his own people don't), is crystal clear whether one interprets it as a sort of parable or as literal history.

Jonah 3:10—Jonah said Nineveh would be destroyed, but it wasn't. Was he wrong?

Some of God's promises read unconditionally yet may be invalidated by human faithlessness, as God explains in Jeremiah 18:7-9. Some are written in absolute terms, as immutable decrees or promises, and yet they maintain a certain flexibility. Jonah himself was less flexible and in fact preferred death to seeing God forgive foreigners (Jonah 1:12; 4:3,8-9). So in a sense, Jonah *was* wrong—about God. In the words of the eminent rabbi Abraham Joshua Heschel, "God is compassion, not compromise; justice, though not inclemency. The prophets' predictions can always be proved wrong by a change in man's conduct, but never the certainty that God is full of compassion."[8]

Micah 1:3-4—Does this refer to the end of the world?

Cosmic language often crops up in oracles promising local punishments or blessings. In Micah 1, the context demands application to Judah, the southern kingdom (1:1,15; 7:4). When God comes, the kingdoms of the earth are shaken (Habakkuk 3:6; Haggai 2:6,21), the mountains melt like wax (Psalm 97:5; 144:5; Amos 9:5; Micah 1:4; Nahum 1:5;). Often he rides the skies on his cloud-chariot (Psalm 68:4,33; 104:3; Isaiah 19:1; Matthew 24:30). These figures point beyond themselves to the ultimate day of judgment. Yet despite the universal language, local judgments are most immediately in view.

Zechariah 14:12—Does Zechariah envision a nuclear war?

No passage in the Bible clearly foretells a nuclear war. This passage, full of apocalyptic images, speaks of plague, not nuclear explosion.

Malachi 3:10—Should we tithe?

Malachi 3:10 addresses Jews living under the law, as does Jesus' comment in Matthew 23:23. If such texts fully apply to us, we should also be tithing on our garden herbs. And yet we do not live in an agricultural society or return 10 percent of the increase of our crops, flocks, and herds to the levitical priesthood.

The early church did not enforce a tithe. In later centuries, in contrast, the tithe became a sort of tax. On the other hand, giving 10 percent is probably a good starting point for most of us in first-world countries. Why don't more people give 10, 20, or 30 percent? Perhaps we've wrecked our lives with credit-card debt and are just trying to get out of the hole. Or we may be living beyond our means, buying things we don't need with money we don't have to impress people who don't care about us anyway.

How much you give is up to you. Do what you feel God wants you to do. Do it cheerfully, not under compulsion. Honor the Lord with your wealth (Proverbs 3:9).

Malachi 4:2—Was Jesus simply another man-made "sun god"?

Malachi 4:2 does in fact compare the Messiah to the sun. Yet the Bible clearly describes the sun as part of the created world (Genesis 1:16), neither divine nor to be worshipped (Ezekiel 8:16-17). The illustration in Malachi is only an analogy. In fact, the early Jews and Christians would never have worshipped a celestial body. The Roman *Sol Invictus* (unconquered sun) was later equated with Christ at a time when paganism was leaking into the church, but this was long after the New Testament was written. Occasionally some aspects of the lives of pagan gods and goddesses parallel Jesus Christ, but that is exactly what we should expect: The counterfeit imitates the authentic.

Part 3

QUESTIONS ABOUT NEW TESTAMENT BOOKS

8

Matthew

Matthew 1:17—Matthew says there were 14 generations from the exile to Jesus, but there are only 13.

Quite a few have pointed out the discrepancy. Like many ancient genealogies, this one is stylized, with numbered groupings and skipped generations. The operative number is 14. The Hebrew Scriptures refer to the kings Jehoiakim and Jehoiachin as *Jeconiah*, so the Greek version (which the early Christians used) applied this word to both Jehoiakim and Jehoiachin. Matthew's Gospel comes to us in Greek and uses *Jeconiah* to represent two kings, not one. Thus Matthew lists 14 generations (inclusive) from the exile to Christ.

Matthew's genealogy traces Jesus' line from Abraham through David, showing that Jesus is the fulfillment of God's promises to the Jews. In contrast, Luke's genealogy contains a "perfect" 77 generations (Luke 3:23-38), extending all the way back to Adam. This intimates that salvation is for the whole human race.

Matthew 1:18-25—Was Mary really a virgin when Jesus was born?

There are many ancient myths about religious leaders having virgin births, as is well known to students of world religions. Here are some examples: Attis, Genghis Khan, Horus, Krishna, Perseus, and Romulus. Of course, the New Testament writers could have been communicating something about the Son of God in terms comprehended by them but not by us. Yet most Christians take the virgin birth at face value. Or, as C.S. Lewis put it, this is a *true* myth—it really happened.

Matthew 1:25—When was Jesus born?

Even the early Christians admitted that they had no idea which month Jesus was born in. Yet the Bible does give a few clues. Shepherds were in the fields with their sheep. This rules out the rainy season (November to March). Besides, the government was conducting a census, which for some odd reason involved families traveling to their ancestral villages. This would have been difficult in the winter, and certainly December. Actually, December 25 was the "birthday" of the Persian god Mithras, which by transference became Jesus' birthday—though not till the third century. It doesn't look too good for the traditional date. But we really don't know. Therefore, you are free to celebrate it whenever you like. Why not every day?

Matthew 3:11—What did John mean when he said of Jesus, "He will baptize you with the Holy Spirit and with fire"?

The baptism of fire is not an experience anyone should seek. Fire is a constant metaphor for judgment and purification throughout Scripture. As John said, "The axe is already at the root of the tree." The fire is none other than the fire of judgment. John seems to be saying that we can be baptized (positively) in water in this age (Mark 1:4; 1 Corinthians 12:13), or we can be immersed (negatively) in the lake of fire in the age to come (Revelation 20:15).

Matthew 3:15—Why did Jesus have to be baptized?

John's baptism conferred forgiveness of sins (Mark 1:4). But Jesus was sinless, so his immersion certainly didn't forgive his sins. Jesus fulfilled the law (Matthew 5:17), yet as a faithful Jew, he did not shy away from the ritual cleansings required by the law. Why did Jesus observe the Passover—to remind himself that he once was lost but now was found? No, but to fulfill all righteousness. His baptism is best understood in this light.

Matthew 4:24—Is demonic possession actually just epilepsy?

Many unknown phenomena were attributed to the demonic in ancient times, yet the Scriptures do not fully support the notion that epilepsy was equated with possession. Matthew 4:24 uses two different words to describe the demon-possessed and the epileptics—*daimonidzomenos* and *seleniadzomenos*. The biblical writers seem to have been clear about the difference between epilepsy and possession.

Remarkably, God apparently protected his people from demon possession in the Old Testament. Yet immediately before the Messiah entered the world, Satan apparently was granted greater liberty. Demon possession afflicted many, and combating it was part of the early apostolic ministry (Luke 9:1).

Matthew 5–7—What is the Sermon on the Mount?

It is the collection of Jesus' teachings that appears in Matthew 5–7.

Matthew 5:22—Jesus himself called people fools. Why isn't he subject to the fire of hell?

Throughout the Sermon on the Mount, Jesus focuses on the inner life, on the attitudes of the heart. Some parts of his teaching are not to be taken literally:

- Gouge out your eye and cut off your hand (5:29-30).
- Divorce makes your wife an adulteress (5:32). Are there

never circumstances under which divorce is justified? (Really? Think about it.) Isn't the Lord stating a stark general truth to challenge the soft commitment of his day and the law-evading tendencies of the flesh?

- Don't take oaths (5:34). Is his intention that we must never swear in court or sign legal documents, or is he simply intending that we be men and women of our word?

- Give to the one who asks (5:42). If a stranger asks me for my house, should I turn over the deed to him? Is this God's purpose for us—that we all quickly become poor? The answer can be yes only if we only understand Jesus' words literally.

- Pray in an inner room (6:6). But did Jesus ever pray indoors, as far as we know? Is he not rather pointing us to correct attitudes and motives for prayer?

- Anger toward a brother (5:22)—our specific topic. Does this mean that if we ever lose our tempers or become angry we will burn in hell? Or is the Lord warning us of the soul-destroying perils of hatred, bitterness, and lack of forgiveness?

God is concerned about our inner attitudes, and we should be too.

Matthew 5:32—Does remarriage constitute adultery?

Adultery is the breaking of faith with one's marriage partner, violating a covenant. This verse is not a prohibition against remarriage except in the case of an adulterous partner. Some interpreters would forbid divorce from a man who is physically abusive, even murderous, provided he hasn't committed adultery. The innocent one is coerced to remain in a physically or psychologically perilous situation, or in the event of separation or divorce, forbidden to have a fresh start in a new relationship. This hard-line view misunderstands that Jesus was overstating his point and using hyperbole to underscore the importance and permanence of the marriage vow. The ultraliteral interpretation produces a legalism every bit as severe as that of the Pharisees. It prevents people from moving on in the wholeness Christ offers.

Matthew 5:44—Does the command to love our enemies preclude the possibility of war?

These are waters seldom plowed by the vessels of biblical investigation. Under the old covenant, church and state were one, and on some occasions warfare was tolerated or even commanded (Deuteronomy 20). But Christ is speaking interpersonally, not politically. He even resisted people's effort to make him a political leader (John 6:15; 18:36).

Jesus tells us to be charitable toward our enemies. In Matthew 7:12 he adds that we are to do to others as we would have them do to us. This means Christians should never abuse, kill, or otherwise harm their relational enemies. Rather, we are to forgive our enemies or pray for them. This was a colossal change from the way of institutional Judaism (Esther 8:13; Psalm 139:21-22; Matthew 5:43). Accordingly, many early Christians chose to be killed rather than to kill their enemies.

Consider the example of Martin Luther King Jr. Does anyone doubt the influence for good of his pacifistic civil rights movement? Or take Nelson Mandela. He effected real change only after being imprisoned and renouncing violence. However, what governments do is very different from what individual Christians do. A number of highly respected Christian thinkers have believed the New Testament calls us to pacifism, including Greg Boyd, Shane Claiborne, Dorothy Day, Stanley Hauerwas, Richard B. Hays, Dwight L. Moody, Leo Tolstoy, Walter Wink, and John Howard Yoder.

Of course the real question is, what did Jesus say about how we are to treat our enemies? The ancient church believed that to pray was of greater value than to kill.

Mathew 6:9—Why does the Bible refer to God as a male?

We will best grasp grace when we allow the Bible to speak for itself. The gender of the pronouns that are used is irrelevant. In Swedish the word for *person* is *människa*, which is feminine. Are we to treat other people as though they were women?

God is not sexual. God is, strictly speaking, neither male, female, nor androgynous (both at the same time), but his image is reflected in both male and female. Does that mean we should not think of God as male? Every passage in the Bible that bears on the subject encourages us to relate to God as a father. Even those passages that employ feminine imagery, such as Matthew 23:37 or Isaiah 66:13, where God deals with his people with the care and compassion of a mother, never teach us to address him as a mother.

Jesus himself addressed God as Father, and he taught us to pray, "Our Father." Several passages imply that masculinity by itself falls short of the mark, as does femininity (1 Thessalonians 2:6-12, for instance). *He* is probably the best pronoun to use because by analogy we are *all* in a feminine relationship to the Lord; he is our husband (Isaiah 54:5; Ephesians 5:22-32). This common biblical metaphor is also evident in Jeremiah, Hosea, and Revelation.

Matthew 6:13—Does God tempt us?

God tempts no one, according to James 1:13. *Tempt* in Matthew 6 is a translation of the same Greek word used in James 1. Yet words are often used different ways in different passages and contexts. There are at least two meanings of *tempt*:

- to test in order to prove, refine, or strengthen

- to entice in order to break down people's resistance so they will give in to sin

The Lord's Prayer uses the first sense of the word. We will be tested in this sense, but we pray that we would not be overwhelmed. God's solid promise of 1 Corinthians 10:13 stands. He will not test us with greater pressure than we are able to endure.

Matthew 6:16—Should Christians fast?

The Didache, an early Christian document used to train disciples, does indeed mention fasting. The Bible never commands Christians to fast, yet Jesus assumed his hearers would fast.

The Catholic practice of a Wednesday and Friday fast—common by the third century—was eventually commuted to abstinence from meat (fish was an allowable exception) on one day a week. Christians did become fond of fasting (as in the Lenten period), yet in time they also became fond of calling men *father*, forbidding marriage, worshipping relics, and worshipping Mary as the queen of heaven. The question boils down to this: Which is more authoritative, the Bible or the church?

Matthew 7:1—Should Christians avoid judging others as lost?

Judgmentalism is never right, and a mere "fire and brimstone" gospel isn't the gospel of Jesus Christ. But the Bible commends some types of judging while condemning others. Here are some wholesome examples of judging:

- *Discerning who is receptive to the gospel* (Matthew 7:6; 10:11-16). It is not unkind to judge who is open to the gospel message and who is not. It's what is fairest to all—both to the person at hand as well as to others who may be seeking the Lord (7:7).

- *Making an assessment about something* (Acts 4:19). The act of judgment itself is neutral. The usual Greek verb for *judge* or *discern* is *krinein*. It is not an inherently negative word. It means moving from premises to conclusions, assessing a situation, discerning, and the like. The spiritual man makes all sorts of judgments (1 Corinthians 2:15).

- *Disciplinary judgment* (1 Corinthians 5:12-13). Church discipline requires that action be taken when serious sin is affecting the congregation, including the expulsion of the unrepentant.

- *Judging disputes* (1 Corinthians 6:1-6). This requires judgment (discernment). The apostle assumes that Christians have the collective wisdom to settle their own disputes instead of going public.

- *Interpreting the Scriptures* (1 Corinthians 10:15; 11:13). We are all encouraged to correctly study and interpret God's word.

These are some of the unhealthy types of judging:

- *Hypocritical judging* (Matthew 7:1-5; Romans 2:1). This is the kind of judging most people have in mind when they express the judgment that one should not judge. Jesus tells us to get the log out of our own eye so we can see clearly enough to help our brother.

- *Superficial judging* (John 7:24). Get the facts and know the Scriptures. That is the only way to make a right judgment. The entire book of Proverbs exhorts us to this sort of practical wisdom.

- *Passing judgment on matters of opinion* (Romans 14:1). We must all take stands on crucial issues, but it is wrong to judge others on the basis of peripheral issues. (In this case, the disputable matter concerns foods.) Accepting the weaker brother doesn't necessarily mean leaving him in a state of ignorance or weak faith. Yet the Lord will hold all of us accountable for how our words affect others (Matthew 12:36).

- *Judging hearts and motives* (1 Corinthians 4:3-5). This is problematic. Yes, out of the mouth comes the overflow of the heart, so we may have some clues as to what is going on in someone's heart or mind. Yet only a person of understanding can draw out the innermost intent (Proverbs 20:5). Paul adds that he does not even judge himself. Let's not get tied in knots trying to analyze everybody—including ourselves!

- *Criticizing* (James 4:11-12). Grumbling—for example, rich Christians complaining against poor Christians, or vice versa—is wrong. We are not to judge others in a critical, destructive manner. Our words should build others up, not tear them down (Ephesians 4:29).

- *Doctrinal nitpicking* (Colossians 2:16). The central teachings of Scripture indicate the core doctrines; not all biblical teachings are equally important. We should "draw the line" only for key doctrines, such as the "seven unities of the faith" in Ephesians 4:3-6.

- *Final judgment* (Acts 10:42; Romans 14:10-12). This is God's prerogative and his alone. To sentence people to heaven or hell is to make a final judgment. No human has the authority to send any other human anywhere after death.

The common plea, "Judge not!" is a gross oversimplification. We all must make many judgments every day. Let's be sure we're doing so in the right spirit.

Matthew 7:12—What is the Golden Rule?

Certainly, it's not "He who has the gold makes the rules," as in the popular quip. The Lord said, "In everything, do to others what you would have them do to you." For the opposite attitude, see Judges 15:3,11. For reference, the "Silver Rule," which is more common among other religions, says we ought not do to others what we would not want them to do to us. Though both rules are demanding, there is a world of difference between them. Jesus' standard is divinely high.

Matthew 9:9; Mark 2:14—Are Matthew and Levi the same person?

They are one and the same. Jews commonly had both a Hebrew name (such as Levi or Saul) and a Greek or Roman name (such as Matthew or Paul).

Matthew 10:23—Why did Jesus say he would come before the 12 completed their mission? Does this contradict Matthew 24:14?

The Lord was encouraging his apostles to keep working till the end—but not, in my opinion, the end of the world, which of course would come long after their lifetime. Divine "coming" in the Bible refers to judgment, to be sure, but only rarely to the end of the world. Through the Roman armies, the Son of Man *did* come back in AD 70 in judgment on Israel, destroying the temple and thus putting an end to the sacrificial system completely. This is what Jesus prophesied in Matthew 10. The apostles and those they influenced were still assiduously carrying out their mission to the Jews when the "end" came— the end of Israel. This does not mean that Jesus won't come again or that we don't need to prepare for the last judgment.

Matthew 11:11-12—Are the kingdom of God and the kingdom of heaven the same thing?

Matthew writes for a predominantly Jewish readership, so he prefers *kingdom of heaven*. He follows the Jewish custom of avoiding the word *God* out of reverence. Mark and Luke show no such hesitation. The phrases are equivalent. (The Gospel of John uses "kingdom" only in Jesus' conversation with Nicodemus [chapter 3] and Pilate [chapter 18].)

Matthew 12:40—Jesus was in the tomb two nights, not three, wasn't he?

You and I do not count the way the ancients did. We nearly always count exclusively; they nearly always reckoned inclusively. The Bible incorporates several chronological schemes that are different from ours. Jesus rose "on the third day" (Matthew 16:21; 17:23; 20:19; Luke 9:22; 18:33; 24:7,46) *and* "after three days" (Matthew 27:63; Mark 8:31; 9:31; 10:34). The two phrases are interchangeable.

I first confronted inclusive reckoning when I began to translate Latin correspondence. "The fifth day after the first of the month" sounds like the *sixth* day of the month. But no—it's the *fifth*. The ancient Greeks, Romans, Hebrews, and other peoples preferred inclusive reckoning instead of exclusive. In ancient thought, the third day after Friday is Sunday. For another biblical example, compare Esther 4:16 and 5:1.

About the days and nights. We moderns would consider "three days and three nights" to be 72 hours or so, and yet to the Hebrews, a day (usually) means a night and a day. Thus "three days" is equivalent to three nights and three days. It could equally well (as in this case) signify one night, a day, another night, and part of the following morning—scarcely 36 hours.

Matthew 13:55-56—How big was Jesus' family?

According to the New Testament, Jesus came from a family of at least ten. This passage names four brothers and mentions "all his sisters" (implying three or more).

Hundreds of millions of Christians believe that Mary bore only one child—Jesus. To them, Mary's holiness would have somehow been compromised if she ever had sexual relations with a man. Yet the plainest understanding of the Bible is that she had a full quiver of children. The doctrine of the perpetual virginity of Mary also founders on Matthew 1:25.

Matthew 15:21-28—Why would Jesus compare this woman to a dog?

Many have tripped over Jesus' surprising choice of metaphor. In fact, I believe he intended us to. The fact that shocking language remains unedited in the New Testament suggests the early Christians considered the Gospels to be inspired by God; they dared not tamper with them or "improve" them.

Dogs commonly referred to Gentiles and does not seem like an endearing term. However, this is not the normal word for a dog, and it appears in the New Testament only here and in the parallel version (Mark 7:24-30). *Kunarion* is the term for a domestic dog, a house dog—the kind that your children play with. It could even be translated as *puppy.* This is not the stronger term used in Philippians 3:2 and Revelation 22:15.

We cannot hear the tone with which Jesus spoke. Was he playful in his speech, or was he serious? This should cause us to be somewhat tentative when drawing conclusions. Obviously Jesus is not connecting women with dogs—gender is not in view here. This woman is going to be an exception to the rule that the gospel would be offered to Jews first (Matthew 10:5-6) and to Gentiles only later (28:19).

Matthew 16:18—Is Peter the rock on which Jesus is building the church? Is he the first pope?

Matthew may have written his Gospel in Hebrew or Aramaic, though this is uncertain. Many Bible teachers contrast *Peter* (Greek: *petros*—stone) with *rock* (Greek: *petra*—bedrock), indicating that the rock is actually Peter's confession of Christ and not Peter himself. The wordplay doesn't even work in Hebrew or Aramaic (as it doesn't in English).

At any rate, Peter was not a pope by any stretch of the imagination, but that does not mean that Jesus isn't designating him a leader of the early church. Without conceding the papacy, I feel comfortable with the idea that Jesus is not contrasting Peter's present unreliable nature with his future, more mature reliability. Rather, Jesus was probably indicating that Peter was indeed the one through whom Jesus would initially launch a world-changing movement. Jesus even entrusted Peter with the keys to the kingdom, which Peter used to open the door to both Jews (Acts 2) and Gentiles (Acts 10).

By the middle of Acts, Peter no longer seems to head up the Jerusalem church. Rather, he shares the leadership with John and James the brother of Jesus. There is no solitary human leader of the worldwide church in the New Testament. And as for apostolic succession, continuity between the ancient and modern church is not based on a line of ordained ministers (fallible and subject to sin), but on apostolic teaching (Acts 2:42). Only the word is perfect. Anyone who picks up the Bible can plant the seed (Luke 8:11) and potentially initiate biblical Christianity—even if the person before him failed to do so.

Matthew 16:18—How could the church become apostate if the gates of hell cannot overcome it?

The Greek text does not read *hell*, but *Hades*. Hell is the location of punishment for those who do not know the Lord; Hades the location of the intermediate state of the dead (believers as well as unbelievers). In this passage, *Hades* refers to death. Even death cannot thwart God's kingdom (Romans 8:38; 1 Corinthians 15:26,54). That is the point, not that the church can never drift away. Even if it did (as Israel did in 2 Chronicles 15:3), new life could spring up after a period of dormancy because the continuity is in the word of God, which is seed, not in the institution of the church. (See the previous entry.)

Matthew 17:10-13—Was John the Baptist a reincarnation of Elijah? And why did John say he *wasn't* Elijah (John 1:21)?

Many first-century Jews expected Elijah to return to the earth literally. In fact, this notion persists in Jewish tradition even today, with the empty seat left for him at the Seder Supper. John did come in the spirit (and clothing!) of Elijah, his ninth-century-BC counterpart (Malachi 3:1; 4:5-6; Matthew 11:10), though in John 1:21 he makes clear that he is not a reincarnation of Elijah. Elijah appeared along with Moses at the Transfiguration (Matthew 17:1-2; Mark 9:2-4; Luke 9:28-31), so how could he have he been reincarnated as John the Baptist? The classic Hindu doctrine of reincarnation requires the rebirth of a dead person, yet Elijah never died (2 Kings 2:11-12). The popular Eastern idea of reincarnation is completely counter to the Bible.

Hinduism has taught reincarnation for many thousands of years. The Chandogya Upanishad 5.10.8 reads, "But those who are of a stinking conduct here—the prospect is, indeed, that they will enter a stinking womb of a dog, or the womb of a swine, or the womb of an outcast." Your status in the next life and the body you will inhabit (canine, porcine, or "untouchable") depend on your conduct in the present life. Eventually all souls "graduate" until *atman* (soul) becomes one with *paramatman* (the world soul). Individual existence disappears. The Scriptures do not allow reincarnation (Job 7:9-10; Hebrews 9:27); it is ultimately part of an impersonal worldview.

Matthew 17:24-27—What was Jesus' real reason for paying the temple tax? He didn't seem to be concerned about offending the Pharisees.

Let me say at the outset that I do pay my taxes and so should you, not just to avoid offending people, but because it's right (Romans 13:6-8). The New Testament mentions two taxes—those paid to the Romans and those paid to the temple and priesthood.

Jesus does not fully accept the legitimacy of the Jewish religious system, which explains why the only reason he pays the tax is to avoid offending others. We, however, file our taxes because they are legally due. Notice that the coin pays the tax for Peter and Jesus both. Unlike so many leaders of the day, Jesus did not make an exception for himself. There was one standard. There is still just one standard.

Matthew 19:10-12—Did Jesus encourage people to refrain from marriage?

According to Jesus, marriage isn't for everybody. Paul too says celibacy is a gift (1 Corinthians 7:7). Not everyone has this gift. If you do, you should seriously consider refraining from marriage. If you don't, you should feel free to seek to be married.

Matthew 19:24—What did Jesus mean by "the eye of a needle"?

Many preachers claim this phrase refers to a rope passing through a needle, a carpet needle, or a gate in Jerusalem (which a camel could not pass through unless it was on its knees). These colorful sermon illustrations were devised long after Jesus' famous comment. Jesus is not saying that entering the kingdom is *difficult* if we're saddled down with worldly priorities and concerns, as was the man in the story. He is saying it's *impossible*. We all know it is impossible to thread a camel through a needle. If Matthew wrote in Aramaic, perhaps the original word was *rope*. That seems plausible (and the words are similar). The point of the passage is clear: Beware materialism.

Matthew 22:37-38—Is there a difference between a disciple's purpose and a disciple's mission?

A Christian's *purpose* is to know God, whereas his *mission* is to bring Jesus to the world. Practically, our mission is to meet people's needs, both spiritual and physical. Some say our sole purpose is to bring others to Christ. Yet reducing it all to how many people you bring to Christ is to lay disproportional emphasis on one teaching of the Bible (as vital and urgent as this need is) and leads to an imbalance that ultimately treats people as objects instead of as persons. The Great Commission (Matthew 28:19-20) isn't optional, but the greatest commandment (Matthew 22:37-38) is more important still. See also the comments on 2 Corinthians 5:21.

Matthew 23:2-35—Why is Jesus so harsh with the Pharisees in Matthew 23?

Jesus' feelings about the Pharisees are clear (Matthew 5:19-20; 15:3-9; 23:1-4). These are only generalizations; out of some 6000 Pharisees in Israel (Josephus, *Antiquities* XVII, 2.4), a number put their faith in Christ. With these the Lord enjoyed an amicable relationship. See also the comments on Matthew 5:22.

Matthew 23:35—Jesus mentions Zechariah son of Berekiah (the postexilic prophet), but he seems to be referring to Zechariah son of Jehoiada (2 Chronicles 24:20-21).

Critics (and most biblical scholars) claim that Jesus (or Matthew) was mistaken about the name of Zechariah's father. He must have meant the son of Jehoiada, who was killed in the temple. Yet several considerations must be taken into account:

- The Old Testament mentions several Zechariahs, and several men were killed near the altar of the temple.

- Zechariah the son of Jehoiada, though mentioned in 2 Chronicles 24:22 (the last book of the Hebrew Bible), is not the last Zechariah chronologically. If Jesus is making a sweeping statement, the span would more likely be from Abel (the first righteous man murdered) to Zechariah (one of the final figures of the Old Testament, who lived around 500 BC), not from Abel to the son of Jehoiada (eighth century BC).

- The New Testament refers to other executions that are not recorded in the Old Testament (see, for example, Hebrews 11), yet this does not mean they never took place.

Jesus did not get his facts wrong, nor did Matthew put erroneous words into Jesus' mouth. Zechariah is linked with Abel because the two represent the righteous persecuted of the Old Testament chronologically, from first to last. That's the link.

Matthew 24:15—What is the abomination that causes desolation?

Here is my take. Jesus is referring back to Daniel 9:27; 11:31. Whether the abomination was originally a pagan image set up in the Most Holy Place or the sacrificing of swine flesh on the altar of the temple, it was an idolatrous desecration of the temple. On this scholars agree.

In the mini-apocalypse of Matthew 24, Mark 13, and Luke 21, Jesus prophesies the desecration of the temple in AD 70 at the hands of the Romans, paralleling the similar desecration which took place two and a half centuries earlier at the hands of Antiochus Epiphanes IV (predicted in Daniel 11:31 and fulfilled in 1 and 2 Maccabees). So the abomination has to do with the desecration of the temple at the hands of pagans.

This does not directly relate to our day because the temple was destroyed long ago, but it was significant in the first century, when Jesus predicted the end of the Jewish sacrificial system. His stunned disciples could scarcely fathom that the temple, in all its glory, could be slated for destruction. But Jesus warns them to flee when they see this omen. History records that this is precisely what those who accepted Jesus' words did. They fled to the town of Pella and thus escaped destruction in the First Jewish War (AD 66–73).

Matthew 27:5—Did Judas hang himself or fall headlong (Acts 1:18)?

We can harmonize the accounts in several ways, yet I would like to make a different point. The fact that it is challenging to harmonize Matthew and Acts is a testimony to the integrity of the early Christians, who chose not to tidy up the two accounts, but to leave them intact. Even in the newspapers today, firsthand accounts of identical events often differ. We need not discount the event because of variations in minor details.

Matthew 27:25—Isn't this a case of Christian anti-Semitism? Would the Jews have said such words?

Yes, I believe they would. Their request for Jesus' death is solemn, like an oath. They are saying, in effect, "We know what we are doing and take responsibility." Of course, the Bible does not portray the Jews as the enemies of God or "Christ-killers."

- The earlier speeches in Acts, addressed to the Jewish leadership, did charge them with a terrible crime. Yet we are all responsible for Jesus' death; he died for mankind's sins, Jews and Gentiles alike (1 Corinthians 15:3; Hebrews 2:9).

- God extended an offer of forgiveness to the Jews (Acts 2:38; 3:17-26), and thousands accepted it (Acts 2:41; 4:4; 21:20).

- The phrase *the Jews* (commonly used in John's Gospel)

usually refers to the Jewish leadership, those most responsible for the crucifixion of Christ. Jesus threw himself on
the wheels of the establishment and was predictably done
away with.

- That generation was punished for their rejection of the gospel in AD 70, when the Romans permanently destroyed
the temple, disbanding the Old Testament system of priesthood and sacrifice. The request of Matthew 27:25 was
granted in the First Jewish War.

- Matthew himself was a Jew writing a Gospel for fellow Jewish Christians. The New Testament is not anti-Semitic.

Matthew 27:62-66—Jesus' tomb was sealed and the guard posted on Saturday. Could Jesus' body have been taken Friday night?

Yes, the seal was placed on the tomb on Saturday. But the guards
likely double-checked the inside of the tomb because they would have
been responsible if someone absconded with the body. But more interesting is the implication for the authenticity of the passage. If the church
had created the resurrection story from whole cloth, why wouldn't they
have the guard and the seal placed on Friday? This attests to the honesty
of the evangelist, for he would have served his purposes better by not
leaving the body untended.

9

Mark and Luke

Mark 1:4—What was the purpose of baptism before Jesus' death and resurrection?

John's baptism prepared people for the coming of the Lord in the spirit of Malachi 3:1; 4:5. John the Baptist paved the way for Jesus' mission by insisting that people be reconciled to one another as a prerequisite for getting right with God. The association of water and forgiveness derives from the Old Testament (Exodus 29:4; Leviticus 14:6; Numbers 19:7; Isaiah 1:16). John's baptism brought people near to God through the forgiveness of sins (Mark 1:4). The nucleus of Jesus' original followers came from the ranks of John's movement.

Mark 1:35—Should we get up early to pray in order to follow the Lord's example?

Jesus constantly depended on the Father. If the Scriptures reflect his daily habits, then perhaps he had no set time for prayer. Besides early morning, he also prayed in the daytime (Luke 11:1), at night (Luke

22:41), and even all night long (Luke 6:12). Although daily prayer is a salutary practice, there is no law to be extracted from the life of the Lord. (But of course, why *wouldn't* anyone want to communicate with the Father on a daily basis?)

Mark 3:29—Is an isolated instance of blaspheming the Spirit an eternal sin?

Paul admits he was a blasphemer and attempted to force others to blaspheme (Acts 26:11; 1 Timothy 1:13), so he would be a good candidate for having committed the eternal sin. And yet the Lord forgave Paul. Regardless of what we have done in our past, forgiveness and genuine hope are in reach (1 Corinthians 6:9-11).

The context is also significant. In Mark 3, religious leaders, who had personally witnessed Jesus' identity and authority, continued to refuse to believe. This demonstrates a hardness of heart from which there was no recovery (Proverbs 29:1). Apparently, when Paul was a Pharisee and church persecutor who strove with all his might to oppose the gospel, he had not "crossed the line"; he had not hardened himself irretrievably. We should resist the urge to "play God," to guess who has and who has not committed the eternal sin.

Finally, the sin is *eternal* because of its consequences in the next age. In Greek (as well as in Latin), the words *age* and *eternal* are related as noun and adjective. *Eternal* carries the sense not so much of infinity as of the world to come. We cannot reject and refuse God in this life and expect a share in the world to come.

Mark 4:31—Why would Jesus say a mustard seed is the smallest seed?

In Greek, *smallest* can well mean *very small*. Besides, the superlative need not be taken literally; hyperbole is common in Semitic parlance. Of course, if Jesus didn't care about relating to his Palestinian audience, he could have named the eucalyptus, whose miniscule seed produces a tree that could be more than 200 feet tall. But he didn't, presumably for the same reason the Bible never mentions koala bears and kangaroos—these were entirely unfamiliar creatures.

The mustard seed is minuscule, and yet it produces a plant up to ten feet tall. The sense is as follows: "The mustard seed—the smallest seed you've ever seen—illustrates what the kingdom of God is like…"

If people are eager to disprove the Bible and discredit Jesus, there may be little you can say to convince them. They have to be willing, in their innermost being, to follow truth wherever it leads (John 7:17). Still, it is good and right to answer criticisms with a to-the-point, respectful explanation.

Mark 6:3—How do we know Jesus was a carpenter?

Jesus was the eldest son of Joseph, the husband of Mary. Joseph was a *tekton*—a woodworker or master craftsman. (Our word *architect* derives from the Greek *archon* [chief] and *tekton*.) Though never explicitly stated in the Bible, it is reasonable to assume from Mark 6:3 that Jesus was a professional craftsman too.

Mark 9:47-48—Does hell last forever? Are people conscious and tortured for all time?

Jesus was quoting from Isaiah 66:24 as he warned about the finality of judgment. But I think Jesus has been misinterpreted, and many scholars, for example John Stott and Edward Fudge, also hold the following opinion.[9] The worm never dies and the fire is never quenched in the vivid imagery of Isaiah. An unquenchable fire would burn up whatever was thrown into it. The *people* in the fire are not conscious; they are just corpses (Isaiah 66:15-16,24; Jeremiah 31:40; Ezekiel 28:18-19). This is no depiction of infinite torment. The emotion evoked is one of disgust, not pity. How different from the medieval picture of hell!

Hell does last forever; there is no escape, no reversal. Yet the fire ultimately destroys those thrown into it (Matthew 10:28). Sooner or later their punishment and consciousness—whether after seconds, months, or millions of years, who can say?—come to an end.

Mark 10:45—To whom did Jesus pay a ransom?

The ransom is also mentioned in Matthew 20:28; 1 Timothy 2:6; and Hebrews 9:15. Technically, the ransom is paid to Satan, not the Father. The devil had become our owner, our new master due to our own sin. He held us hostage. The ransom is always paid to the one who holds the hostage—to the bad guy, not the good guy. Anselm (AD 1033–1109) popularized the idea that the ransom was paid to God. This interpretation is widespread and dominant, but we can take these passages another way.

In The Chronicles of Narnia, Aslan (the lion, representing Christ) allowed himself to be slain, giving himself into the hands of Jadis the White Witch (representing the devil) and thus freeing her captives. Yet analogies only illustrate—they do not prove anything. Interpret the less clear Scriptures in light of the more clear ones. This is great advice whenever you are tackling the more difficult doctrines of the Bible.

Mark 11:24—Will we really get whatever we want if our faith is intense enough?

Broadly speaking, such thinking is called word-faith theology. In short, if you believe it (or "claim" it), it will happen. This wrongheaded thinking is based on a misunderstanding of Mark 11:24 and other passages. In essence, if we can only convince ourselves that God will answer our prayers, he will. As a result, we control God. This view is first cousin to the Eastern "mind over matter" teaching. And yet by sheer willpower we can create nothing. Our prayers must be in accordance with God's will, as 1 John 5:14-15 teaches. The view is similar to prosperity theology, which says, "I can get whatever I want if I want it badly enough."

Mark 11:25—Should we stand when we pray?

Yes, standing is good (1 Samuel 1:26; Matthew 6:5). So are kneeling (1 Kings 8:54; Daniel 6:10; Acts 21:5), lying (Mark 14:35; 1 Corinthians 14:25), and sitting (Judges 20:26-28). The most common position in ancient Christian art is standing with arms outstretched (hands lifted—Psalm 63:4). The Bible stresses the inner disposition of the heart much more than the position in prayer (Matthew 6:5-15). That determines our true standing before the Lord.

Mark 13:32—If Jesus is God, how could he not have known when he was going to return?

During Jesus' earthly human existence, he was subject to certain limitations. Obviously he could not be omnipresent while a human; he was spatially bound. The same appears true of his omniscience; as a man, Jesus did not know all things (Matthew 24:36 records this as well).

Mark 14:32–15:37—What is the Passion?

The original meaning of *passion* is suffering. The Passion is Jesus' suffering, particularly from his triumphal entry into Jerusalem to his crucifixion five days later. The word is not used in the Bible in this sense, but it is common in the literature of the church.

Mark 15:22—What is Calvary?

Calvaria is the Latin translation of the Greek *kranion,* corresponding to the Hebrew *gulgoleth.* All three words refer to the skull or the head. Calvary, the Place of the Skull, was the site of the crucifixion (Matthew 27:33; Luke 23:33; John 19:17).

Mark 15:24—Is gambling wrong?

The Bible has little to say about gambling—directly, at least. But it has a great deal to say about stewardship. For most players, gambling is poor stewardship. The lottery—one of many get-rich-quick schemes—promises enormous payouts to the winners, yet chances of winning approach the infinitesimal. One person wins, but millions lose. The poor, the elderly, and minorities are the most frequent players. Gambling also breeds indiscipline and financial ruin and attracts organized crime and prostitution. At the risk of oversimplifying, gambling is a poor choice. I personally do not want to have anything to do with it, though other Christians' consciences allow them to participate.

But back to stewardship. God is not a cheapskate. In Mark 14, we see Jesus' reaction to those who criticized a woman for "wasting" expensive perfume on him. On the other hand, he does hold us accountable for thoughts, words, and actions (Psalm 19:14; Matthew 12:36; 2 Corinthians 5:10; Hebrews 4:13). Many parables show that the Lord expects wisdom in our use of money and possessions (Luke 10:25-37; 12:13-21; 16:1-15; 18:18-29).

Of course, there are degrees of gambling, or of taking various risks. For instance, would it be irresponsible for a man who makes $100,000,000 a year to buy a raffle ticket? (Are you sure?) Let's refrain from being judgmental and strive to speak only where the Bible speaks. Base your convictions on God's word, remembering lessons from your own experience and conscience.

Mark 15:26—What did Jesus' cross look like?

The upright post was likely fixed in the ground. Jesus carried the crossbeam (John 19:17), though with help (Matthew 27:32; Mark 15:21; Luke 23:26). The *titulus* specified his crime and was appended to the top of the cross. The Gospel accounts indicate the traditional cross shape, not a Tau cross.

Mark 15:33—Who was Thallus, and is his account of Jesus' death and resurrection reputable?

Thallus was a freedman of the emperor Tiberius. He wrote a history of Greece and its relations with the states of Asia Minor, from the Trojan War to his own day. In book 3, he refers to the darkness covering Palestine during Jesus' crucifixion. Thallus reasoned that this was due to an eclipse. That is impossible, however, since Jesus was crucified at Passover, when the moon was full and on the wrong side of the earth. At any rate, Thallus did live closer to the time of the crucifixion than

[handwritten annotation: Christian theologians →]

the patristic writers, so his mention of the period of darkness is significant (Matthew 27:45; Luke 23:44).

Mark 16:17-18—Does Mark 16 encourage Christians to handle snakes?

Mark 16:9-20 was appended to the original Gospel by copyists. In this passage, Jesus refers to believers not being harmed by snakebites. Such happened in Acts 28:3-5 when Paul was attacked by a viper but suffered no ill effect. There is no biblical requirement of handling poisonous snakes in order to prove one's faith, yet some do it all the same. How do they explain the adverse effects they sometimes experience?

- God is punishing sin.
- God allows the bite to prove the snakes are in fact deadly.
- God is testing people's faith.
- God is providing an opportunity to show his healing power.

For those whose minds are made up, such serpentine rationalizations explain everything.

Luke 1:1-4—What is the document referred to as Q? If it's authentic, why isn't it included in the Bible?

In this passage, Luke mentions that he used various sources. If the source theory is right, Matthew and Luke both used a document called *Q* (for the German *Quelle*, or "source") to supplement their primary source document, the Gospel of Mark. In other words, most of the traditions and sayings from the life of Jesus that occur only in Matthew and Luke originate from *Q*. This means that much of *Q* actually did find its way into the New Testament.

Luke 1:48—Should we venerate the Virgin Mary?

Despite the honor she is due, when Mary uttered, "From now on all generations will call me blessed," I doubt she had in mind the cult of the Virgin as we know it. The Council of Ephesus voted that Mary was the Mother of God (AD 431) and later added that she was taken bodily into heaven to reign as queen of heaven (1954). These are certainly developments not anticipated in Scripture (except negatively, as in Jeremiah 7:18; 44:17-19,25).

In the early Middle Ages, on account of an uneasy (and biblically fallacious) sense that Jesus was stern and inaccessible, emphasis shifted to his mother. Apparitions are common in human history. Kwan Yin, Chinese goddess of mercy, has appeared to many, as has the Phrygian Mother Goddess and Buddhism's Avalokiteshvara. And so has Maria, besides a plethora of other "saints." Goddesses have always been popular, and in their absence, religions tend to invent them.

Luke 2:1—Who was Caesar Augustus?

The Caesars were the supreme leaders of Rome, named after Gaius Julius Caesar (100–44 BC). His grand-nephew Caesar Augustus was the first emperor and ruled when Jesus was born. Tiberius was Caesar when Jesus was crucified.

Following is a list of Caesars and their dates from the beginning of the Roman Empire to the time of Constantine, when the church and state contracted their fatal marriage alliance. Each has an interesting story, and there is no shortage of books about these leaders of what was once the most powerful empire on earth.

Caesars Through the Ages (abbreviated list)	
Augustus 27 BC–AD 14	Caligula 37–41
Tiberius 14–3	Claudius 41–54
Nero 54–68	Caracalla 211–217
Galba 68-69	Elagabalus 218–222
Otho 69	Alexander Severus 222–235
Vitellius 69	Maximinus Thrax 235–238
Vespasian 69–79	Gordian III 238–244
Titus 79–81	Philip 244–249
Domitian 81–96	Decius 249–251
Nerva 96–98	Valerian/Gallienus 253–260
Trajan 98–117	Gallienus 260–268
Hadrian 117–138	Claudius II 268–270
Antoninus Pius 138–161	Aurelian 270–275
Lucius Verus 161–169	Probus 276–282
Marcus Aurelius 161–180	Diocletian 284–286
Commodus 180–192	Diocletian & Maximian 286–305
Septimus Severus 193–211	Constantius & Galerius 305 (AD 431)

Luke 2:1-2—Was Quirinius really governor of Syria during this census?

Quirinius probably didn't become governor of Syria until AD 6. Was Luke wrong? Many solutions have been proposed:

- Perhaps Quirinius served two terms as governor or even governed Syria earlier from the geographical location of his previous post. Interestingly, Tertullian (in the late second century) places the nativity census in the governorship of Saturninus (9–3 BC).

- Some suggest an alternate translation: "This registration [census] happened *before* Quirinius was governor of Syria." This is possible, because AD 6 was a significant year—that's when Palestine reverted to direct Roman rule.

- Perhaps Herod was finally obliged to order the census when Quirinius was a special *Legatus Augusti* to Syria (6 BC), invested with the command of the army and entrusted with its foreign affairs. Quirinius stood in exactly the same relation to Varus, the governor of Syria, as at a later time Vespasian did to Mucianus. Vespasian conducted the war in Palestine while Mucianus was governor of Syria and Vespasian was *Legatus Augusti,* holding precisely the same title and technical rank as Mucianus. This is an intriguing possibility, though speculative.

- An error has crept into the text in the copying process, though the original wording was presumably correct.

To be honest, I do not find any of these suggestions particularly satisfying. Yet whatever our solution, we ought to take into account Luke's accuracy in points of geography and history. Luke uses about 200 terms—technical names for individual people, cities, islands, bodies of water, and the like—and as far as we know, he never makes a mistake. Someone with such a high degree of credibility and proven accuracy should be presumed correct unless what he wrote cannot possibly harmonize with other known facts.

Luke 2:7—What color was Jesus' skin?

He was not white. Or black. As a Middle Easterner—like Abraham, Moses, and David—he had a dark complexion. And yet we know nothing else about his appearance, though we may surmise one thing from his betrayal. Judas directed the arrest party to Jesus by a kiss

(Mark 14:44). If Jesus was beardless, or was especially tall, or bore a halo, or was otherwise different from his contemporaries, Judas could have simply described him or pointed to him. Yet Jesus seems to have blended into the crowd; his appearance was ordinary, not extraordinary. There you have it: an ordinary man, though darkly complected. All our spiritual ancestors were "people of color."

Luke 2:41-51—What happened to Joseph?

Joseph's absence during Jesus' adult years is conspicuous. Most commentators believe Joseph died before Jesus' public ministry began. This would make sense of Jesus' entrusting his mother to the care of a friend (John 19:26-27). Why would he have done this if Joseph were still alive? Presumably Jesus' four younger brothers were married and all had their own families, so "the disciple whom he loved" was more available. The fact that Jesus had seven or more siblings (Matthew 13:55-56) proves Joseph did in fact have relations with Mary. This is also the natural reading of Matthew 1:25.

Luke 2:52—Did Jesus ever go to India?

There is zero evidence that Jesus ever visited Tibet or India, though the idea is popular among followers of the New Age Movement; some Muslims also hold that Jesus settled in India and died there after becoming a centenarian. Only around 35 days of Jesus' life are recorded in Scripture, but the story is complete enough to convince us that he never left Israel except when his family fled to Egypt to escape Herod. The family business, not to mention the probable early death of his father, kept Jesus at home all the way up to the start of his public ministry around AD 27. At any rate, he could not have received his teaching directly from the Buddha, who died five centuries before his time.

Some people minimize and soften the exclusive claims of Christ by comparing and even blending his teachings with other religious traditions. This will not do. Jesus Christ alone is the way, the truth, and the life.

Jesus ministered in an area of about ten thousand square miles—an area about the size of Massachusetts and less than 1 percent of 1 percent of the planet—but what an impact!

Luke 3:23—Why did Jesus wait until he was 30 to start his public ministry?

Luke says Jesus was *about* 30. If he was born before the death of Herod the Great (Matthew 2:1), his birth could have been no later than 4 BC (the year of Herod's demise). Herod's attempt to kill all Bethlehem boys two years and younger (Matthew 2:16) seems to place Jesus' birth no later than 6 or 5 BC. We know that Jesus began his public ministry about AD 27.

- Luke 3:1-2 says John the Baptist was active about AD 27–28
- Tiberius began to reign in AD 14
- Pilate began to serve as Prefect of Judea in AD 26

Therefore, Jesus' crucifixion would have taken place in AD 30. All of this to say that we know nothing of Jesus' life from infancy until AD 27 (except for the trip to Jerusalem when he was 12—Luke 2:41-52), a gap of some 20 years. Why the delay?

- *Family responsibility.* Joseph apparently died much earlier than Mary. As eldest of at least eight children (Matthew 13:55-56), Jesus would have become the head of the family. Call it love, call it filial piety, call it honoring father and mother...Jesus was the one to take responsibility for the family. At some point, his brother James probably took over.

- *Credibility.* Might the people of Israel have struggled to take seriously a Messiah still in his teens or twenties?

- *John's ministry.* John the Baptist was the prophesied forerunner of the Lord (Isaiah 40:3-5; Malachi 3:1-2; 4:5-6), so Jesus waited for his herald.

- *Character formation.* The Scriptures do not teach that Jesus emerged from the Jordan—much less the womb—with his character fully formed. Hebrews 5:8 shows that Jesus *learned* through the suffering process. This was not restricted to the final few days of his earthly ministry. Life is replete with opportunities to suffer, and growing through them was an integral part of the Incarnation itself. This may be the most significant reason for the delay.

- *Time.* Closely related to the previous reason, character formation requires testing over a period of time. No one would be ready to pilot a plane after a single flying lesson. People are considered trustworthy after years of weathering storms and patiently enduring trials.

- *Professional experience.* Learning a trade (carpentry, or construction, as the Greek word suggests) gave Jesus enhanced credibility, "relatability," and the life experience he so frequently drew from in his teaching ministry.

Luke 6:13—What's the difference between a disciple and an apostle?

Disciple means "student"; *apostle* means "missionary." Sometimes the 12 apostles are called disciples because they were Jesus' original followers. All Christians are disciples (Acts 11:26), but not all disciples are apostles (Ephesians 4:11).

Apostles were eyewitnesses of the resurrected Jesus, who chose them to carry the gospel to the world as his emissaries (Acts 1:22; 1 Corinthians 9:1). Paul joined the apostolic group two or three years after the start of the church. Having served to establish the church (Ephesians 2:20), apostles no longer exist today, at least in the restricted sense of the word. Some people besides the 12 were called apostles in the broader sense of "missionaries" (Acts 14:4,14; Romans 16:7).

Luke 7:28—In what sense was John "greater"? Who is the "least in the kingdom of God"?

Greater does not refer to John's passion, heroism, accomplishments, or popularity, for few will match him in any of these. *Greater* pertains to position. John, in one sense, did not participate in the kingdom, whereas later followers of Jesus do (Colossians 1:12-13). Those who lived and died under the old covenant (Jewish law), like John, experienced their relationship with God less directly than we do (Ephesians 2:18; Hebrews 11:40). Most important, under that covenant, the indwelling Spirit was not given to believers. This happened only after Jesus' ascension (John 7:39-40).

Luke 9:23—What does "take up his cross daily" mean?

The image of someone carrying his own cross was common enough in the first century, when public executions by crucifixion left an indelible imprint on the mind. The connection of the cross with death was thus inescapable. As Jesus and others teach, we are to be willing to die and also to put sinful behaviors to death (John 12:24-26; Romans 6:6; Galatians 2:20; 5:24; 6:14; Colossians 2:20; 3:1,5). This attitude is meant to shape our lives daily. The cross impacts our lifestyle in practical ways.

Luke 9:27—In what sense did the kingdom appear before Jesus' hearers died?

Several suggestions have been made, pointing to the gift of the Spirit at Pentecost, or to the destruction of Jerusalem in AD 70, or to the end of the world. Regarding the first option, Pentecost was only a few weeks in the future, so a prediction that *some* would not die before then would not be much of a prediction.

The second option fits with Matthew's parallel account, which indicates a day of judgment: "For the Son of Man is going to come in his Father's glory with his angels, and then he will reward each person according to what he has done. I tell you the truth, some who are

standing here will not taste death before they see the Son of Man coming in his kingdom" (Matthew 16:27-28). In AD 70, the Jerusalem
temple and the entire sacrificial system were formally destroyed by the
Romans—the Lord came in judgment.

Jesus' words also apply (more broadly) to the last judgment, following
the Lord's coming. Anytime God demonstrates his regal power, we may
say the kingdom is coming. When the king comes, the kingdom comes.

Luke 9:28-36—What was the purpose of the transfiguration, and why were Elijah and Moses included?

This revelation of Jesus' divinity—his heavenly glory—makes his
earthly suffering (Luke 9:23-27) all the more remarkable. The transfiguration also shows us that the ministry of Jesus (the gospel) is comple-
mentary to, yet also superior to, the ministries of Moses (the Law) and
Elijah (the Prophets). This event is also referred to in Matthew 17:1-8;
Mark 9:2-8; 2 Peter 1:16-18; and perhaps John 1:14.

Luke 9:57-60—What does "let the dead bury their own dead" mean?

Don't worry if this passage disturbs you—Jesus intended it to. He
is trying to get our attention. This verse is not telling us whether we
should or should not attend funerals. Was the father still living? That
too is immaterial. The point (expressed hyperbolically) is that God's
kingdom, his sovereignty, comes before all else. And all of us have a difficult time with that.

Luke 12:33—Are we really to give away all our possessions?

Jesus is stressing the need to remain unattached to material possessions. The rich are commanded to share (1 Timothy 6:17-19). If they
have given away everything, they would no longer be rich—or even
able to share. Only one rich man, as far as I know, was told to sell everything (Luke 18:22). Which of your possessions should you liquidate
and when? These are decisions you alone should make.

Luke 12:47-48—Will there be degrees of punishment and reward? Isn't Christ's gift of salvation complete and based on grace?

I once resisted the notion of treasure in heaven even though Jesus taught it himself (Matthew 6:20). I felt such an emphasis might encourage wrong motives. Yet eventually I changed my mind because I came to the conviction that this is what the Bible teaches. Degrees of reward, or treasure in heaven, do not nullify God's grace or the completeness of our salvation. The Bible clearly teaches that we will be judged according to what we have done (Matthew 16:27; Romans 2:6; Revelation 22:12). Our service is not only a response to salvation but also an identification with Christ (Philippians 2:12; 3:10-11; Colossians 1:24).

To modify the common comparison with the judgment day, the exam is not just pass/fail. Letter grades are given as well. As we follow Christ, the refining fires of personal sacrifice and the opposition of the world continually purge us from being unduly governed by hope of reward. For more, see the comments on 2 Corinthians 5:10.

Luke 14:26—In what sense are we to hate our families?

Hate in this passage seems to correspond to loving less in Matthew 10:37 (see also Genesis 29:30-31). But a better solution is found in Luke 16:13, where Jesus says no one can serve two masters. He will love (serve) one and hate the other. *Hate* in both passages is a hyperbole—a common feature of Semitic speech.

Luke 16:1-9—Is Jesus sanctioning dishonesty? Is he encouraging us to buy friends?

Most parables have one main point. Here it is the urgency of the hour. Even pagans know how to hustle, how to get going when times are desperate. To enter into the kingdom and live in it, we need to be just as resourceful, just as determined.

Luke 16:23—Was the rich man in hell, or is this just a parable?

I take the story, which was familiar in antiquity, as a parable, but its historicity has no bearing on the truth Jesus is teaching. Besides, Jesus doesn't picture the rich man as being in hell, but in Hades, as the NIV footnote indicates. He was in the underworld, already beginning to experience his ultimate punishment (2 Peter 2:9). This contrasts with Lazarus, who was in Abraham's bosom (a common term for paradise), enjoying the comfort that would be his after the judgment day. Consider the words of the early Christians:

- "The souls of the godly remain in a better place, while those of the unjust and wicked are in a worse place, waiting for the time of judgment" (Justin Martyr, 1.197).

- "No disciple is above his master...Our master, therefore, did not at once depart, taking flight [to heaven]. Rather, he awaited the time of his resurrection, as determined by the Father...Likewise, we also should await the time of our resurrection determined by God" (Irenaeus, 1.560-561).

- "The rich man was in torment and the poor man was comforted in the bosom of Abraham. The one was to be punished in Hades, and the other was to be comforted in Abraham's bosom. Yet they are both spoken of as before the coming of the Savior and before the end of the world. Therefore, their condition is before the resurrection" (Methodius, 6.377).

- "Let no one imagine that souls are immediately judged after death. For all are detained in one and a common place of confinement—until the arrival of the time [of] the great Judge" (Lactantius, 7.217).[10]

The rich man and Lazarus were in separate compartments of Hades (the underworld). For more, see the comments on John 3:13; 14:3; and 2 Corinthians 5:10.

Luke 17:20-21—What is the kingdom?

A kingdom requires a king (leader) and kingdom (territory or rule). Most believers do not envision the kingdom of God as a political or geographical entity, though some incline in that direction. Jehovah's Witnesses claim that Jesus came to earth to set up the kingdom but failed. Here are some more reasonable explanations.

- In one sense, the kingdom is the entire universe. God's reign is universal; everyone is in it regardless of whether he or she wants to be.

- More specifically, the kingdom is the domain of the King's rule; it comprises the willing subjects of the King. On earth this has special meaning for the church. The church is not the kingdom, but the kingdom includes the church, the corporate body of those who submit to Jesus as Lord.

- More specifically still, the kingdom was especially present in the personal ministry of Jesus Christ (Matthew 12:28).

When we become Christians, we become part of the kingdom (Colossians 1:13); now our citizenship is in heaven (Philippians 3:20).

Luke 22:36—Jesus tells the 12 to sell their cloaks and buy swords. But when Peter uses his sword, Jesus tells him to stop (John 18:10-11). Why?

This passage has been the source of much lively discussion in the past two millennia. A few commentators think Jesus advocated carrying arms, yet most think he was simply (but emphatically) warning the disciples of coming persecution. This was William Barclay's interpretation.

> Jesus was saying, "All the time so far you have had me with you. In a very short time you are going to be cast upon your own resources. What are you going to do about it? The danger in a very short time is not that you will possess nothing; but that you will have to fight for your very existence." This was

not an incitement to armed force. It was simply a vivid Eastern way of telling the disciples that their very lives were at stake.[11]

As so often happened, the disciples misunderstood Jesus' words and took them literally. He chides them and heals the man whose ear Peter lopped off. Violence was not the way of the Master.

Luke 22:44—Did Jesus sweat blood literally or figuratively?

I was taught—and used to teach—that Luke was describing the rare phenomenon of *haematridosis*, or bloody sweat. Yet nothing in the text says so. "Like drops of blood" seems to refer to the *way* in which the sweat was pouring from Jesus' body. Have you ever had a gash? Remember how quickly the blood dripped out? Jesus' sweat fell to the ground like blood issuing from a deep wound. The doctrine of bloody sweat is not warranted.

Luke 24:6—Was the ascension the same day as the resurrection or 40 days later (Luke 24:50-51; Acts 1:3-9)?

At first blush, the Gospel does appear to indicate that the ascension and resurrection took place on the same Sunday. But keeping in mind that Luke wrote both the Gospel of Luke and Acts—where the ascension is 40 days after the resurrection—we must give him the benefit of the doubt. Scripture often telescopes events. That is, in one breath it mentions events that may take place days, years, or even centuries apart. Perhaps Luke ends his Gospel with the ascension because this is how he will begin the book of Acts; the ascension is the transition between volumes 1 and 2 of his magnum opus.

10

John and Acts

John 1:1—Are Jesus and the Bible both the Word?

The Word (*logos*) of John 1:1 and the word (Bible) are related, but they are not exactly the same. In Jesus we see God (John 14:9; Colossians 2:9), and in him the message (or word) of God dwells (John 1:14). God also speaks to us in his word. That is why John refers to Christ as the Word. Naturally the Scriptures, which speak to us of God and reveal the incredible story of which every one of us is part, are also described as a word from God. In the incarnation, God takes on human flesh. In the Bible, the word of God comes to us in human words. So when Christians speak of Jesus Christ as the Word of God, and the Bible as the word of God, they are talking about different realities. Yet there are many connections. For example, Proverbs 8:1–9:6 speaks of God's wisdom, which is equated with Christ in 1 Corinthians 1:30. He was an agent in creation at the very beginning (see also Colossians 1:15-17). Thus we see that Jesus and the Bible, though separate, are connected. The Scriptures, after all, are his story.

John 1:14—Which Bible passages show that Jesus is God in the flesh?

This verse is one of the clearest. The Word became flesh; and this Word is God (compare with verses 1 and 18). Here are a few more passages: Philippians 2:6; Colossians 1:15; 2:9; Titus 2:13; Hebrews 1:8; 2 Peter 1:1. The theological term for God becoming man is *Incarnation*, which could also be rendered *enfleshment*. It is the greatest miracle of the Bible, in which Almighty God takes on humanity, spanning an infinite chasm to reach you and me, Creator reaching out to creature.

John 1:49-51—Did Nathanael see angels ascending and descending on the Son of Man?

Nathanael realized Jesus is the Son of God, the King of Israel. *Son of Man* was the messianic title Jesus used when referring to himself (Daniel 7:13). Jesus is alluding to Genesis 28:12, in which Jacob dreams of angels in transit between heaven and earth. Jesus implies that he is the stairway to heaven, the way to the Father, as he makes explicit in John 14:6.

John 2:4—Was Jesus rude to his mother?

In the NASB, the verse reads, "Woman, what does that have to do with us? My hour has not yet come." *Woman* is the same term Jesus tenderly used in John 19:26 when he provided for Mary's care after the crucifixion. No disrespect was intended by his question, and it probably didn't come across as brusque in the original language as it does in English. In fact, Jesus complied with her request by providing more wine without allowing himself to be manipulated or the timing of his divine actions to be accelerated.

John 2:13-22—Did Jesus suffer a fit of violent rage? And when did this occur?

In Psalm 4:4 and Ephesians 4:26 we read, "In your anger do not sin," or alternately, "Be angry but do not sin." The Bible distinguishes between righteous anger and a fit of rage (selfish anger). Jesus' action is calculated. God's anger follows his great patience, and the Scriptures repeatedly describe the Lord as slow to anger.

On one hand, anger is not always ungodly. On the other hand, this passage is not a proof text for violent political action. (Notice that Jesus didn't cleanse Herod's palace or Pilate's residence or the Sanhedrin. As the house of God, the temple stood in a unique category.)

As for when this piece of prophetic drama took place, we should note that the ancient writers' approach to chronology was different from ours. The cleansing happens at the end of Jesus' public ministry in Matthew, Mark, and Luke. John, however, has moved it to the beginning, grouping it with other material related to the contrast between the old and the new. Such thematic grouping of material is common in ancient histories. Where chronology mattered, as opposed to theology, Bible writers carefully demonstrated historical awareness and accuracy (Luke 2:1-2; 3:1-2).

John 2:14—Why were people exchanging money in the temple in the first place?

Some worshippers brought animals to sacrifice; others bought them, especially when they lived too far away to bring their own (Deuteronomy 14:24-26). The sellers made a commission. In time, the service the sellers provided degenerated into profiteering.

John 3:13—Has no one gone into heaven, or did that change after Jesus' ascension?

In the Bible we do not see anyone in heaven or hell because Jesus has not returned, the dead have not been raised, and judgment day is still future (John 5:28-29; 11:24; 12:48; 14:3). In Acts 2:34 Peter noted that David had not yet ascended to heaven, and in fact for several centuries all Christians believed that the dead wait in the underworld (Sheol or Hades) for the last resurrection. This means that no one dies and immediately goes to heaven. We die and wait in anticipation of our final destiny.

John 3:16—Why is John 3:16 the Bible verse we always see on posters at sports events?

This verse touches hearts because it demonstrates God's loving initiative toward us. And yet it omits the details of how we are to accept the good news. No one will come to God without accepting the truth about Jesus and taking him at his word (1:12; 12:48). In addition to faith, a full response includes repentance and baptism (3:5). Becoming a Christian is not a private experience, but a public event, a true conversion from darkness to the light (3:19-21).

John 3:18—What happens to people who never hear the gospel?

According to this passage, those who do not believe are in trouble. If those who don't know about Jesus could be saved, evangelism wouldn't be essential. Yet Jesus, who knew we would do less than a perfect job, commanded us to make disciples of all nations. No one will be saved by being a nice person, for all have fallen short (Romans 3:23). Thus it is imperative that we get the word out. People aren't lost because they haven't heard the gospel, but because they are in sin.

As for ancient peoples without access to the Scriptures or the Hebrew prophets (who addressed a number of Middle Eastern nations), Gentiles learned about God only through nature (Acts 14:16-17; Romans 1:18-20), conscience (Romans 2:14-15), and the experience of following or violating God's universal moral law (Romans 1:32). Yet this should not be taken to mean they could be saved by works—by reaching some minimal standard of God-consciousness or just being decent persons. Romans 2:12 explains that those who sin apart from the law are still guilty—and all sin.

Ancient cultures were characterized by sin as much as we are today: ritual prostitution, cannibalism, ecological irresponsibility, revenge, and human sacrifice. Though liberal sociologists, anthropologists, and artists often glorify primitive peoples, we should be leery of the argument that ancient cultures were closer to nature and goodness than we are. All have sinned and fallen short, as Paul argues in Romans. The religious and the irreligious, Jew and Gentile alike, are all lost and can only throw themselves on God's grace (Romans 3:23-24).

John 4:24—What does "worship in spirit and in truth" mean?

Some interpret *spirit* as zeal and *truth* as correct doctrine. Others see *spirit* as a reference to the Holy Spirit. As vital as these factors are, such interpretations do not fit the passage. The key to understanding the passage has to do with the ongoing dispute between Jews and Samaritans.

Jews believed Mount Zion, the site of the temple, was the closest a human could come to the presence of God. Yet the Samaritans, whose origin can be traced to the eighth century BC (2 Kings 17), held that Mount Gerizim was the best place to worship. Their rival temple had stood there until it was destroyed in 129 BC. Rewriting the Decalogue, the Samaritans added a commandment requiring God's people to worship him on *their* mountain.

Jesus' point seems to be that God is no longer accessed spatially (geographically), but spiritually. The entire world is now a single hot spot, or "spiritual Wi-Fi" zone. Anyone may approach the Lord anywhere, anytime. As for *truth*, the Lord is confronting the Samaritan woman in love, encouraging her to be honest about her life. *Truth* is a synonym for *authenticity*.

John 5:28-29—When Jesus returns, will there be two separate resurrections?

Jesus taught that there will be *one* moment when all the dead will exit their graves, good and evil alike. Revelation 20:5 is sometimes interpreted as supporting two separate resurrections, superimposing the image of the millennium on the image of resurrection. (See comments on Revelation 20:1-6.) Whatever this apocalyptic text means—and it is embedded in a passage fraught with symbolism—it should not be read in a way that contradicts Jesus' more prosaic words in John 5. Nor does 1 Thessalonians 4:16-17 shore up the two-resurrection theory;

some may rise before others without there being separate events. (We may be not all be admitted to the theater simultaneously even if we are all attending the same performance.) Daniel 12:2 also describes a single resurrection.

John 10:16—Who are the other sheep Jesus mentions?

The other sheep are the Gentiles. The mystery of the gospel was that the Gentiles would ultimately be blessed along with the Jews (Genesis 12:3; Ephesians 3:4-6).

John 11:35—Is this the shortest verse in the Greek manuscripts as well as the English translations of the Bible?

Edakrusen ho Iesous, "Jesus wept," is the shortest verse in most English Bibles, but in the Greek New Testament, the winner is Luke 20:30 (*kai ho deuteros,* "and the second"), which in Greek is 12 letters. This is followed by *Pantote chairete,* "Always rejoice" (1 Thessalonians 5:16), 14 letters in two words. First Thessalonians 5:17, pray continually, is also two words in Greek, but it contains 22 letters. Another memorable passage is "Remember Lot's wife" (Luke 17:32).

In the Hebrew Old Testament, the shortest verse is *'Ever, Peelg, R^eu,* "Eber, Peleg, Reu" (1 Chronicles 1:25), which in the original language is nine letters in three words.

John 13:23—Who is the disciple whom Jesus loved? And did he write the Gospel of John?

This nameless character appears only here and in John 19:26; 20:2; 21:7,20. Or is he nameless? Some scholars propose the anonymous disciple is Lazarus, who was certainly a close friend to Jesus (John 11:1–12:2, especially 11:36). Once Lazarus' life is in jeopardy (John 12:10-11), he vanishes—right as "the disciple Jesus loved" enters the stage. This hypothesis has much to commend it. The weight of tradition supports John as the author, but we must remember that all four Gospels are anonymous documents.

John 14:3—Will we be judged immediately at death (Luke 16:23) or later (Matthew 25:31-46)?

Luke 16 does not describe existence after the judgment, but before. Most Bible readers imagine that the dead go to heaven before Christ's second coming, but John 14:3 says otherwise.

I wrestled with this question for ten years and resisted the view I now accept. (All of us must do our best to interpret the Scriptures in a way that makes sense to us, and this may involve a prolonged period of time.) It is also the view of the early church, and has been taught in modern times by such British scholars as John Stott and N.T. Wright and also popularized by Christian writer Randy Alcorn.[12] I now understand the sequence of events to look like this:

death→Hades→second coming→resurrection→final judgment→heaven or hell

After we live, we die (once; there is no reincarnation—Hebrews 9:27). Those who are lost don't need to wait until the judgment to find out where they stand. They stand condemned already (John 3:18), and their punishment begins even before the judgment (2 Peter 2:9). On the other hand, the redeemed, like the penitent thief, go to paradise—but paradise is not heaven. Recall that on Good Friday, Jesus told the thief he would see him in paradise that very day (Luke 23:43), whereas on Easter Sunday he told Mary Magdalene he had not yet ascended to the Father (John 20:17). The conclusion is this: *Paradise* is not necessarily a synonym for *heaven*. In fact, for the early Christians, it typically meant the part of Hades populated by the redeemed.

Between our death and resurrection, we are conscious. Sleep is a metaphor for death (John 11:11; 1 Corinthians 15:51). Luke 16:19-31 supports this view. Lazarus is in paradise (the metaphor is "Abraham's bosom"), and the rich man is in agony. They can see each other. Hades is the underworld (*Sheol* in the Hebrew Old Testament) and includes good and bad compartments.

Though we may chafe at the idea, Jesus insisted that no one has gone into heaven except the one who came from heaven (John 3:13). Peter confirmed this, saying that not even David ascended to heaven (Acts 2:34). The term *paradise* is not always used technically, and it occasionally refers to heaven (Revelation 2:7), but the picture of the next world that emerges from the Old and New Testaments forces us to distinguish paradise from heaven. Jesus taught that we will not go to the Father until he returns (John 14:3). One day he will return for us, but this has not yet taken place. When he comes back, the dead will hear his voice and rise (John 5:28-29).

After our resurrection, we appear before the judgment seat of Christ. This judgment is declarative, not investigative. God is not trying to figure out whether we are going to be admitted to heaven; he already knows. He merely pronounces officially what our destiny is. The righteous will then go to heaven—not before. The lost will be destroyed in the fire, which is called the second death (Revelation 2:11; 20:6,14; 21:8).

The upshot is that believers who have passed on are in paradise, conscious and happy. They await the Lord's return, when they will be taken to heaven. This explanation harmonizes all the Scriptures, requires no Einsteinian space-time speculation, and is in accord with the teaching of the church during its first three centuries. Hades is only a layover on the way to our true destination. For now, heaven must wait.

John 15:2,4-5,8,16—What is the fruit we are to bear?

Some people equate bearing fruit with leading others to Christ. But John 15 is much broader than this. *Fruit* has at least eight meanings in Scripture.

1. children (Genesis 17:6-7)
2. signs of repentance (Matthew 3:8)
3. the effect of someone's life (Matthew 7:16; John 15)
4. literal fruit, such as figs and grapes (Matthew 26:29; Luke 13:7)

5. a relief contribution (Romans 15:28)

6. virtues (Galatians 5:22-23; Ephesians 5:9) and vices (Romans 7:5)

7. church growth (Colossians 1:6)

8. worshipful praise (Hebrews 13:15)

Fruit in John 15 is productivity in an evangelistic context. The more New Testament fruit we bear, the greater the harvest of evangelistic fruit is bound to be. We may play different roles in that process (1 Corinthians 3:5-9), yet we are all under obligation to live out the gospel, embracing a lost and dying world, just as God in Christ reached out to us.

John 19:14—In Matthew, Mark, and Luke, Jesus celebrates the Passover with his disciples, but in John, they ask for his body to be taken down before the beginning of Passover. How do we explain this?

The celebration around Passover time actually lasts eight days and includes the Feast of Unleavened Bread (Exodus 12:15-18). Thursday night the disciples consumed the Passover meal. The main part of the festival started the day following. Jesus was crucified on Friday. The Sabbath began several hours after his death, and Jewish law forbade leaving a corpse on a tree after sunset (Deuteronomy 21:22-23).

However, Matthew 27:45 does in fact differ from John 19:13-14. In Matthew's account, by the sixth hour, Jesus had been on the cross for some time, whereas in the Gospel of John he is still before Pilate on the Stone Pavement. The evangelists were following different time-keeping systems. Matthew, the most Jewish of the four Gospels, uses the Jewish system. The sixth hour is midday, and Jesus died at the ninth hour, or three in the afternoon. John, on the other hand, writing for a non-Jewish audience, follows the Roman system, which is our own. The sixth hour was six in the morning.

John 20:22-23—What does Jesus' breath indicate? And how does his mention of forgiveness relate to Matthew 16:19?

This dramatic action indicates that the apostles were to receive the Spirit. It seems to tie in with Matthew 16. The apostles (who were already right with God—John 15:3 says they were clean because of the word Jesus had spoken) received special abilities other believers do not possess (Luke 9:2; John 14:26; 16:13; Acts 2:43). The apostles never remitted sins on earth, as Jesus did in Mark 2:5,10-11. Jesus helped those under the old covenant to get right with God. From Pentecost on, the apostles helped people to be saved through the new covenant (Acts 2:38,42; 8:31-38; 16:31-32; 26:20).

John 21:15-17—Does the original language shed any light on the repeated use of the word *love* in this passage?

The original exchange would have taken place in Aramaic, not Greek, so Jesus might not have distinguished between these two verbs for *love*. If the passage has a deeper meaning, it lies in Jesus' three questions to Peter and Peter's three denials of Jesus. The connection between loving the Lord and loving others is also significant.

In John 21, *agapas me* (love as an act of will and commitment) and *phileis me* (love as an act of devotion based in the affection) are synonymous. This means Jesus is probably not asking Peter if he is his friend. To illustrate, *philein* is the verb used in Matthew 10:37; John 11:3; 20:2; Romans 12:10; 1 Corinthians 16:22; Titus 2:4 (twice); 3.15. On top of all this, *philein* describes God's love for the disciples in John 16:27. And several other examples could be cited.

For a parallel, compare James 4:4 to 1 John 2:15. The first speaks of friendship with the world, the second of love for the world. Yet the meaning is the same. So in John 21 there may be absolutely no difference between these words despite what most preachers say.

Another false distinction from the same passage would be between *arnia* (lambs) in verse 15 and *probata* (sheep) in verses 16 and 17. The words don't have the same root meaning, but in this context they are used interchangeably, in accordance with the dictates of good style.

Acts 1:1—Why is this book called the Acts of the Apostles even though only Peter and Paul feature prominently?

Some have suggested the book ought to be called The Acts of Peter and Paul. Their ministries share several parallels:

1. preaching to Gentiles (Peter in Acts 10; Paul from Acts 9 on)
2. defeating a sorcerer (Acts 8:9-24; 13:6-12)
3. healing a lame man (Acts 3:1-10; 14:8-10)
4. raising the dead (Acts 9:36-42; 20:7-12)
5. healing the sick indirectly (Acts 5:15; 19:11-12)
6. imparting the Spirit (Acts 8:14-17; 19:1-7)
7. escaping from prison (Acts 12:1-11; 16:25-34)

Another suggestion is The Acts of the Holy Spirit because the Spirit is the motivating force, inspiration, director of evangelism, and compelling presence of God throughout the book. Of course, to be technical, Luke wrote both the Gospel of Luke and Acts, so this book might most accurately be called The Continuing Acts of Jesus Through His Church by the Power of the Spirit. But that wouldn't fit on the title page.

Acts 1:18-19; Matthew 27:3-10—Who bought the field, and whom was it named for?

First, did the Jewish leaders buy the field (per Matthew's account), or did Judas buy it (per Acts)? The answer is both. The Jewish leaders did not feel right about taking the "blood money" into the temple treasury, so they bought a field with it. They *directly* bought it; Judas *indirectly* bought it because the money was his.

Second, is the field named the Field of Blood because foreigners were to be buried there (per Matthew's account) or because of Judas' suicide (per Acts)? Actually, Matthew does not say it was named because of the foreigners buried there. Matthew 27:8 refers back to verse 6, not verse 7. A lot is going on in this field: remorse, suicide, land purchase, fulfillment of prophecy—but no contradiction.

By the way, the place still bears the name *Hakeldama* today.

Acts 1:26—Is casting lots an appropriate way to determine God's will?

Lots were part of the priestly decision-making process under the old covenant (the Urim and Thummim of Exodus 28:30). But we have no warrant for extending the practice today, nor do we find any precedent in the New Testament church, which is not established until Acts 2. It would be handy, wouldn't it? *Oui, monsieur.* (Or would it be Ouija, *monsieur?*) True enough, in Proverbs, casting lots settles disputes (18:18)—like drawing straws. I see no harm in this or in tossing a coin. But this is hardly a way to make important decisions, and it certainly does not divine the will of God.

Acts 2:1—Does *they* in Acts 2:1 refer to the 12 apostles or to the 120 (Acts 1:15)?

Though Jesus had a sizable contingent—500 or more (1 Corinthians 15:6) and 120 in Jerusalem alone (Acts 1:15)—the group of Acts 2:1 is smaller. They are Galileans (2:7). The immediate antecedent of 2:1 is the previous verse, 1:26, where the full complement of apostles is once again 12. They are still the persons in view in 2:14. It is simplest to understand the group of 2:1 as the 12, not the 120.

Acts 2:14-36—Did Luke paraphrase Peter's sermon in Acts 2:14-39?

Speeches in the Bible are condensed and paraphrased. Biblical writers did not feel a burden to report the exact words. In fact, everything Jesus said that is recorded in the Bible can be read aloud in just a couple of hours. Surely Jesus spoke for more than two hours during his three-year ministry. If the Bible recorded everything he said, the Gospels would be tens of thousands of pages long. I read Peter's Pentecost sermon aloud and clocked myself at two minutes and ten seconds. Are we to believe that the apostle's inaugural message was so brief? Probably not. Besides, Luke himself tells us that Peter spoke "many other words" (Acts 2:40). Further, Peter was probably not speaking in English or even Greek, but in Aramaic. So Luke's Greek rendition does not preserve Peter's original words.

Critics say Luke put words into Peter's mouth. If you've ever told another person that he was putting words into your mouth, you were accusing him of misrepresenting you. But we don't object when others paraphrase, reword, or summarize us, provided our meaning has been preserved. Paraphrasing is not misrepresenting.

Acts 2:38—Are we to baptize in Jesus' name or in the name of the Father, Son, and Holy Spirit (Matthew 28:19)?

These are simply two ways of saying the same thing. *In the name of* means, essentially, "by the authority of." The Bible never explicitly specifies a verbal formula for baptisms.

Acts 2:42—Does "the breaking of bread" refer to receiving Communion or to sharing an actual meal?

The phrase is ambivalent. My take is that 2:42 refers to the Lord's Supper, 2:46 to ordinary fellowship meals. The New Testament (Acts 20:7) and early Christian sources show that the early disciples celebrated the Lord's Supper regularly, probably weekly. People joined around the table for a real meal, not an emblematic ceremony.

Acts 4:32-37—Should Christians share all their possessions and liquidate their assets to support those in need?

Jesus commanded only one would-be follower to give away all his wealth (Luke 18:22). Not even Zacchaeus, who had wronged others, was commanded to give all his wealth away (Luke 19:8-9). Giving away all we own is different from sharing gladly and freely with those in want. The first can be done without love (1 Corinthians 13:3); the second fulfills the Scriptures.

Besides, if we pooled all our possessions, we could no longer help needier members because we'd all be equally needy. The inequality affords room for compassion, generosity, and gratitude. This brings us to an important distinction. The New Testament does not equate the poor and the needy. To say "there were no needy persons among them" is not to say "there were no poor persons among them." Most believers—like most people throughout human history—are poor. In many countries the poor will always predominate. God does require the rich to be generous (1 Timothy 6:17-18), yet he never commands the pooling of resources for a homogeneous standard of living. The needy require assistance for food, drink, clothes, and shelter (Matthew 6:25-34). Jesus Christ's plan for meeting their needs depends on the assistance of the family and the local congregation. Charity begins at home (1 Timothy 5:8) and continues in the home church (Galatians 6:10).

Acts 5:32—Does God give the Spirit only to those who obey him?

God takes up residence in our hearts when we make Jesus Lord, not simply because we feel a spiritual energy or have a religious experience (John 14:15-21). God's love is unconditional, but receiving the Spirit is not (Acts 2:38).

Acts 8:2—What does the Bible say about burial and cremation?

The Bible does not dictate a particular position on this subject. In many cultures, corpses are routinely burned. In most, they are buried. In some, they are intentionally exposed to the elements, allowing the birds to peck away the flesh until only a skeleton remains. Some people request that their ashes be scattered over rivers, mountains, or special places. There is no consensus on the most respectful way to dispose of the bodies of the departed.

Godly men buried Stephen, but not because it would have been against God's will to dispose of the body in some other way. In general the Gentiles practiced cremation, and the Jews opted for inhumation. Many believers, however, are uncomfortable with cremation because they believe such a practice might interfere with our resurrection at the last day. The Bible does, after all, mention a *bodily* resurrection. Our new bodies will be spiritual (1 Corinthians 15:44), but they will be bodies nonetheless.

But if God is able to renew the bodies of the dead, surely he can accomplish this whether the body is drowned (Exodus 15:4), buried in the sand (Exodus 2:12), dismembered (Judges 20:6), eaten by animals (2 Kings 9:34-37), consumed by fire (2 Peter 3:10–13), or even incorporated into the body of another human (see comments on Lamentations 4:10). For nothing is impossible with God (Luke 1:37). Furthermore, we might not honor God more with our bodies in a moldering, decomposing state than in an incinerated one. In the final analysis, the Bible is silent on this issue, so it remains a matter of opinion.

Acts 8:37—Why is this verse missing?

Verse 37 isn't in the most ancient manuscripts, though many ancient writers refer to the Ethiopian's confession, suggesting that it may be a genuine excerpt from the interchange. The manuscripts on which the KJV was based were from the 1400s and 1500s, and they were not always in the best shape. Consequently, the KJV contains hundreds of minor errors. Eventually older Greek manuscripts were discovered— in which this passage is absent—so newer translations omit verse 37. Rather than change the versification, verses 36 and 38 retained their numbers.

The manuscripts on which some of the older English versions relied had gradually gathered accretions—extra words and sometimes even sentences—that do not appear in the oldest Greek manuscripts. These extra words probably do not amount to more than 1 percent of the length of the canonical Scriptures. Modern translations from the original languages are right to omit them, even without a footnote. The insertions in the medieval manuscripts did not introduce new doctrines. They merely reiterated orthodox teaching.

By the way, this new convert is not the first Ethiopian eunuch. There is another in the Old Testament (Jeremiah 38:7).

Acts 15:9—Were Cornelius and his Gentile friends purified by faith alone? What about repentance, baptism, and lordship?

Peter is recounting the events of Acts 10:43-48. The text doesn't say they were saved at the point of belief. Faith purifies the heart, though salvation is a process involving more. Besides, as Peter reminds us, at this point in his message he had only begun to speak (Acts 11:15). He hadn't rounded out the message necessary for salvation. After the miracle from God, he continues (or accelerates) his talk and tells his listeners about forgiveness through Jesus' name (10:48).

Acts 16:3—Why did Timothy allow Paul to circumcise him?

In Acts 15:1,5 we find some Christians from the party of the Pharisees teaching that circumcision and law keeping were essential for salvation. Paul, Barnabas, and Peter strongly disagreed (15:2,6-11), and James and the other apostles and elders followed their lead (15:19).

So when Paul circumcised Timothy, he didn't do it so Timothy would be saved. Had this been his view, he would have circumcised Titus too, but he didn't (Galatians 2:3). In consistency with Paul's principles of outreach (1 Corinthians 9:19-23), he enhanced Timothy's effectiveness among the Jews by removing a potential stumbling block, since Timothy was technically a Jew himself. (He had a Jewish mother.) Titus, on the other hand, was from a Gentile background.

Although Paul was very clear that keeping Torah did not save, he saw no need to renounce his religious heritage and in fact would not hesitate to draw upon it if this allowed him to reap a larger harvest of souls.

Acts 17:26—Does God determine exactly where and when people will live?

The NIV seems to imply that God foreordains everything, down to the finest detail of your life, and that you ultimately have no control. But if that were true, he would then *de facto* be predestining the lost to live in places and during times without access to the gospel. A better translation is the rendering of the HCSB: "From one man He has made every nation of men to live all over the earth and has determined their appointed times and the boundaries of where they live." This is not to deny God's sovereignty, providence, response to prayer, or involvement in our lives.

Paul is explaining to the Athenians that God worked out the geographical and social conditions necessary for creatures made in his image to know him. Therefore we can devote ourselves to finding the truth, to reaching out for the Father.

Acts 19:18-19—Does God require us to confess every sin before he accepts us as Christians?

No passage in the New Testament requires confession of all sins to another human being before conversion. James 5:16 and 1 John 1:9 are for those who are already believers. John's baptism may establish the precedent of confession before baptism, but even then confession is not exhaustive. When we require more for conversion than Jesus and the apostles did, we have gone beyond what is written (1 Corinthians 4:6). Let's be careful that we are not making the narrow gate (Matthew 7:13) narrower or wider than it really is.

Acts 19:18 contains a valuable lesson. Certain sins were brought into the open only *after* conversion. Many sins can be forsaken immediately. Yet despite a genuine initial repentance, through the conviction of the Holy Spirit we become increasingly aware of sin in our lives. This process stretches over many years. Further, some have been so deeply traumatized (through sexual abuse, psychological torment, and the like) that they seem incapable of total openness until they have been following Christ for a few years. It takes time to build trust, and intimate secrets do not readily yield themselves, especially to relatively new acquaintances. Openness and honesty are certainly important, but we should take care lest we require more of a penitent person than God himself requires.

11

Romans to 2 Corinthians

Romans 1:18—Does Christianity build on the foundational truths shared by most religions?

Beginning in Romans 1:18, the apostle Paul explains that certain truths about God may be known from nature. Psalm 19:1-2 contains this same idea. God's design, wisdom, intelligence, and power are obvious in his creation. Furthermore, some truths are universal (concerning murder, adultery, respect for elders, and so on) and require no special word from God. Such truths are matters of *general revelation*. Others, however, cannot be known apart from the *special revelation* provided in the Judeo-Christian Scriptures, in God's workings in the history of ancient Israel, and in the life of Jesus Christ. The former have been shown to all men, regardless of religion, which is why they are "without excuse" (Romans 1:20). The latter cannot be known apart from the Scripture. Read the Bible with your friends from other religions, and they will see soon enough where the Christian message goes beyond the basic tenets of other belief systems.

Romans 1:26-27—What does the Bible teach about homosexuality?

Both Testaments indicate that homosexuality is sinful. God intended marriage to be for a man and a woman (Genesis 2:24), and sex outside of marriage goes against his will. Relevant passages include Genesis 19:5-7; Leviticus 18:22; 20:13; 1 Corinthians 6:9; and 1 Timothy 1:10. Yet as long as our society emphasizes the pursuit of happiness over the pursuit of holiness, the biblical teaching will be eclipsed by rhetoric.

Homosexuality occasionally occurs naturally in the animal world (as among the bonobos), but we are called to rise above the animals, not to imitate them. Of course, homosexuality is unnatural as a matter of biological engineering.

Some people counter that homosexual acts are condemned only in connection with idolatry (1:23). But to be consistent, are all the acts decried in the following verses illicit only when practiced in idolatry? Surely they are wrong whether carried out by Jews or Gentiles, believers or atheists.

Another argument for homosexuality is that it's hardwired into some people's brains. This will not do. Neural pathways develop as we settle into certain behavioral patterns; that is how the Lord made us. Habits thus becomes more and more deeply engrained. A brain scan simply pictures what is there; it doesn't tell us how it got that way *or* what is right. Yet even if there *is* a biological predisposition to a particular sin (gluttony, impulsiveness, laziness, alcoholism, homosexuality), it doesn't justify giving in.

God calls us to master our desires, to develop discipline. I may have been born with a tendency to hot-bloodedness or chemical addiction—and if so, there are mitigating factors—but still I must take full responsibility for my own behavior. Further, the opposite of homosexuality is not heterosexuality, but holiness. The goal is not for a person to be heterosexual—after all, most heterosexuals will not enter the narrow gate—but to live a holy life. We have choices. No one is forced to give in to his or her stronger temptations.

Many have left the world of active homosexuality, finding forgiveness and acceptance in Christ and in his church. Yet such a fresh start is frustrated through heartless denunciations like the one I found on a church marquee: "Homosexuality is a terrible sin." This message was guaranteed to repel seekers from a gay background. Jesus was a friend of sinners, scandalous by virtue of the company he kept. I suspect if he were to come to Atlanta, San Francisco, or Paris today, his loving interactions with gays would draw heavy fire from many conservative Christians.

Romans 1:26—Does the Bible forbid lesbianism?

The Old Testament explicitly forbids only male homosexuality. But an argument from silence doesn't legitimize lesbianism. As a rough parallel, Leviticus 20:15 forbids male bestiality. What if the following verse and Leviticus 18:23 (which condemn female bestiality) were not in the Bible? Would that mean female bestiality was permissible? Of course not.

The New Testament is clear about lesbianism (Romans 1:26). Paul was thoroughly Jewish and certainly shared the common rejection of lesbianism. God's plan for sex is found in Genesis 2:24: One man, one wife, for life.

Romans 5:12—In what way did death enter the world through sin? Death existed before the fall.

Death in Romans 5:12 refers to the human realm. Death must have been a part of God's plan from the very beginning because there are millions of microscopic organisms whose life and death are integral to human physiological function. In addition, God had already given the plants to man for food; therefore botanical death was a reality before the fall.

True, Romans 8:21-22 suggests a connection between Adam's sin and the decay and corruption in the biological world. Maybe the biological world illustrates human corruption, but I don't see how Adam could have brought physical death into the world. I tend to look at the story of the garden as an extended metaphor of our spiritual condition and need for God. Moreover, in Scripture the natural world is often personified. Mountains clap, stones cry out, stars praise God. There is no need to take these passages literally. (See the introduction [page 5], "Are we to read the Bible literally or figuratively? [page 24], and "How should we read the poetry of the Bible? [page 109].)

Romans 7:14-25—Is Paul describing his past or his present struggle to do what's right?

Paul is "fleshing out" existence apart from Christ. Romans 7 illustrates the mind-set of the person trying to be justified on his own. He lacks the power to overcome. Romans 8, on the other hand, illustrates life as it should be, a life that is possible only by the Spirit of Christ. Paul describes the same struggle in Galatians 5. In a nutshell, Romans 7 depicts a frustrating struggle and defeat, but Romans 8 portrays victory, a joyous life through Jesus Christ. We all live in Romans 7 at times, just as in Christ we all have the power to enjoy Romans 8. It's not either-or; it's both-and.

Romans 8:15—Is the Trinity a biblical teaching or a theological extrapolation?

The doctrine of the Trinity is not explicit in the New Testament, but it is implicit. The term was first used around AD 200. We experience the Lord as a triune God—not as three separate gods or as one god appearing in three modes, but as the holy, divine, three-in-one God. We see all three persons of the godhead dynamically involved in several passages of Scripture (Matthew 28:19; Romans 1:1-4; Galatians 4:6; Titus 3:4-6). To put it succinctly, we relate *to* God the Father *through* God the Son *by the power of* God the Holy Spirit.

Romans 8:29—How do predestination and free will fit together?

If free will is illusory, then divine justice is farcical. In Acts 2:36, Peter preaches that the crucifixion took place in accordance with God's set purpose and foreknowledge, and yet his listeners were still responsible. Human free will need not clash with God's sovereign purposes. I took the train from London to Cambridge. As long as I remain on board, I am destined to arrive in Cambridge. I am not forced—I could always jump off at the wrong station because I have free will.

Romans 8 doesn't contradict the principle of free will. Paul is not referring to predestination to salvation, but to predestination to become like Christ. God's plan is that we be conformed to his character through suffering (Romans 8:17). Note also that this is the context of the popular verse 28, which is usually isolated from its context: a radically Spirit-led life.

Romans 11:25-27—Will the Jews be saved just by being God's people?

As I see it, Paul is explaining that only those Jews who follow the Messiah are the people of God (Romans 9:6). The Jews who rejected Jesus were not part of the remnant (9:27; 11:1,5), but those who accepted him, including Mary (the mother of Jesus), Elizabeth, Zechariah, Anna, Simeon, and the apostle himself, were part of the remnant.

Paul is addressing the situation of the Jews in his day, not ours. His readers would not have been comforted if he had said, in effect, "Don't worry about all your (Jewish) friends and relatives; 2000 years from now, all living Jews will accept Christ." These thoughts support this interpretation—that the Jews who would be saved were the Jews of Paul's day. Only a handful of scholars are on my side in this interpretation, but ponder it and see what you think about these points:

- Romans 9:6 defines true Jews as persons of faith. Ancestry is irrelevant. As John the Baptist put it, God can raise up children for Abraham from stones (Matthew 3:9).

- Romans 11:25 reads (literally) "the fullness of the Gentiles," not the "full number," a mistranslation that implies an event still in our future. The same word appears in 15:29. The Gentile mission, in fulfilling key prophecies, was moving the Jews to accept the Messiah. This suggests a first-century fulfillment.

- The natural branches (11:21,24) are the sons of the covenant. See Acts 3:25-26. Modern Jews, even though some are turning to Christ, are no more automatically sons of the covenant than were the Jews in Peter's day. They are no longer "the chosen people," as the kingdom was removed from them (Matthew 21:43) and given to the new people of God.

- The olive tree (Romans 11:24) is not the political state of Israel, but the true people of God. In fact, most Jews in Israel are atheists or agnostics. Unbelieving Jews were never part of the olive tree.

- Those who rejected the Messiah were hardened (11:25) *because* they were unbelievers, not the other way around. They had a choice.

Naturally, as I share my faith with Jewish persons, I *hope* that many will come to the Lord before the curtain of time descends, but it is difficult to support a mass conversion of the nation of Israel from Romans 11. The Jewish faithful remnant accepted the Messiah through the course of the first century. Together with the believing Gentiles, they constituted the true people of God. See further comments on Amos 9:11.

Romans 13:1—Did the founders of the United States sin by rebelling against England?

In light of Romans 13, revolution, regardless of many valid political justifications, cannot be supported biblically. Few citizens of any nation who have fought for liberty have thought this issue through theologically—with the Bible in hand and a willingness to consider the words of Jesus about our enemies. Americans can be proud of some aspects of our country while rejecting the more ignominious facets. Deeming it morally wrong to kill our enemies doesn't make us ungrateful for our nation or unwilling to obey our own government... provided, of course, we aren't asked to do anything contrary to Scripture or our conscience (Daniel 6:6-10). Ah—there's the rub.

Romans 13:1-5—Are we bound to obey senseless laws?

Obsolete, awkward, and illogical laws have a way of going out of existence, officially or unofficially. What is the context of Romans 13? It is referring to paying taxes (verse 6). It is also referring to crimes against the state, crimes that can merit the death penalty (verse 4). These are hardly on the same level as some antiquated laws that simply have not yet been removed from the books.

Romans 16:1-27—Is Romans 16 original? If so, how did Paul know so many people in a city he'd never visited?

Some manuscripts of Romans end with chapter 15. Other manuscripts place chapter 16 between chapters 14 and 15. What happened? I see two possibilities. Perhaps the last chapter was added as a sort of appendix, probably by Paul. Or perhaps in some manuscripts chapter 16 became detached and was later reattached.

And why couldn't Paul know lots of people in a city he had never visited? Missionaries moved around a lot, and Christian relationships crisscrossed the Mediterranean. I know people in a number of places I've never visited—because they moved there after we met, or because we have bumped into each other while traveling, or because we have written letters to one another.

Romans 16:16—Should we greet one another with a kiss?

The question brings up the difference between form and function. The outward form of the greeting (kiss, embrace, handshake) is different from the function (an affectionate display of Christian welcome). Function is more important than form. Moreover, in New Testament times, as today in the Middle East, holy kisses were extended only to members of the same sex. (Just try kissing another man's wife in the Arab world!) A similar line of reasoning can be applied to a few other ancient customs, such as foot washing and daily personal anointing.

1 Corinthians 3:12-15—How can people be saved if their work is burned up?

The context of 1 Corinthians 3 is the building up of the church, not our individual Christian lives (and not purgatory, as the Roman Catholic church claims). Paul seems to be saying that if the foundation you have built for your congregation is unstable, your work will burn up, though you will still be saved. So unless you are a church builder, this test of fire does not apply to you. Not to say that our life's work may or may not have an enduring effect, even if we aren't church workers. Of course it will.

As for whether you can be saved if your life's work does not pass the test—well, we rightly reject salvation by works. God's grace produces in us a rejection of worldliness (Titus 2:11-14) and a determination to work hard (1 Corinthians 15:10), but we do not work in order to be saved. We don't have to measure up. Isn't this good news?

1 Corinthians 5:9—How many letters did Paul write to the Corinthians?

First Corinthians 5:9 and 2 Corinthians 7:8 refer to letters that have been lost. Paul wrote at least four letters to the Corinthians. Letters were a primary means of communication and follow-up. I would not be surprised if the apostle wrote 100 epistles in all, considering that he planted dozens of churches.

Bible students use the words *letter* and *epistle* interchangeably, though there is a slight difference. An epistle has a teaching purpose, but a letter is more chatty and doesn't have a doctrinal agenda. *Epistle* comes from the Latin *epistula* and Greek *epistolé*, both of which mean "letter." Most of the epistles were written before the Gospels.

1 Corinthians 5:11—What behaviors lead to exclusion from fellowship?

Disfellowship is a serious matter, warranted by grave sin without repentance or false teaching (actively trying to turn others from the church), as in Titus 3:9-11. Local leadership makes the call, issuing the notice with love and with sensitivity to any legal implications. Paul specifically refers to people who call themselves brothers. He is distinguishing between a church member and an outsider. (Nonmembers cannot be disfellowshipped because they aren't in the fellowship in the first place.)

1 Corinthians 6:1-8—Is taking a Christian to court always wrong? What about suing a non-Christian?

We can look at Paul's logic in two ways. One is to affirm that suing a fellow believer gives the faith a bad name. Settle internecine disputes in-house; other suits can be taken to the courts. The other perspective is that Christians shouldn't sue anyone at all, so litigation with a brother in Christ is out of the question.

Paul seems to be saying, "Try to work things out, but don't rely on the arm of the state (with its threats of confiscation, incarceration, and execution). Overcome evil with good." In our rights-demanding society, the second perspective sounds strange, and yet this is the understanding that fits more smoothly with other New Testament passages (Matthew 5:38-42; Romans 12:17-21).

1 Corinthians 6:19-20—Does body piercing dishonor God?

The New Testament does not say anything about body piercing. Yet there is a vital principle: Our bodies are temples of the Holy Spirit, and they belong to Christ, not to us. We should not do anything to our bodies that contradicts this principle. Does piercing glorify God or self?

People pierce for all sorts of reasons. It may be the cultural norm, as is often the case in some tribal societies that pierce or stretch lips, ears, tongues, and necks. What would be inherently wrong with this? Other times people pierce their bodies to make a statement. Such actions may be born of insecurity about one's identity. Jesus Christ was supremely confident in his identity and his purpose, and the only obvious bodily statement he made was to humble himself in the Incarnation. Jesus was comfortable with who he was; probably more than any other human being, he understood that God looks at the heart (1 Samuel 16:7).

We do not need to judge the morality of body piercing, as this isn't a moral issue. Nor is it a directly biblical one. But we should check our motives.

1 Corinthians 7:1,7-9,38—Is celibacy better than marriage?

First Corinthians 7 does indeed urge the advantages of remaining single, at least in certain situations. Some singles have the gift of celibacy. We do them a disservice by pushing them to marry, or worse, by teasing them. Marriage is the norm, but it's not for everyone. Jesus and Paul are only two great people of faith who come to mind in this context. Paul states that some of us have the gift of celibacy (7:7). Just as surely as this should never be forced on anyone (1 Timothy 4:1-5), so marriage should never be pushed on anyone who might have the legitimate gift of remaining single.

Luke 20:34-35 says nothing about the status of marriage in eternity. At the resurrection, God will have no problem sorting out the complexities of those who have remarried. Marriage is a valid and honorable institution, as the Scriptures insist (Hebrews 13:4). Should you get married or not? That's your decision.

1 Corinthians 7:12—Was Paul saying this instruction is not inspired?

First Corinthians 7 is a commentary on Jesus' words related in Matthew 19:3-12, where the Lord lays down the law for marriage between two covenant people. Jesus did not teach about the situation between a believer and a non-believing spouse. That was for the Spirit to accomplish through Paul (1 Corinthians 7:10,12,39). "I, not the Lord" doesn't mean Paul doubts his inspiration (as he asserts in verse 40). It means, in effect, "I'm speaking about an issue the Lord did not cover." Similarly, "Not I, but the Lord" is not meant to distinguish between levels of inspiration or authority. It simply reminds the reader that the Lord had already spoken about covenant marriages. Paul is certainly not denying his own inspiration as an apostle.

1 Corinthians 7:14—Are spouses of believers automatically saved?

Paul is simply urging a believing spouse not to separate from an unbelieving one too quickly because this compromises the unbeliever's best chance of becoming a Christian. Whether Paul's reference to sanctification implies potential salvation or special setting apart for the plan of God must be determined from the context of 1 Corinthians. To answer the question directly, an unbelieving spouse *can* be saved through the believing spouse—assuming the believing spouse is patient and doesn't break off the relationship. The unbeliever *can* be saved—but he or she isn't saved yet.

Here's another view on this passage. A spouse in a mixed marriage might be tempted to give up entirely, so Paul is hoping for the evangelistic payoff of patient endurance. He is also saying that the children are clean. This means that they are not illegitimate in the sight of God. Our interpretation of this passage should not lead us to give up on marriages, even when one of the partners is not following Christ.

1 Corinthians 11:6—Why don't most Christian women cover their heads today?

Most Christians today believe this practice was specific to the first-century culture, as were foot washing and the holy kiss. In Paul's day, women in the Eastern Mediterranean world wore veils—pagans and Christians alike. Upper-class women who were eager to show off their coiffure were the exception. For equivalent present-day Western examples, Christian women shouldn't wear plunging necklines in public (demonstrating immodesty) or criticize their husbands in front of others (undermining their God-ordained leadership).

In many countries, women are still veiled, not only to avoid "morals police" but also to prevent lust. In such places, the absence of the covering would hinder the gospel. In other places, the effect would be the opposite; a veil would be a needless distraction. Let's follow Paul's example in 1 Corinthians 9:22 and "become all things to all men" (and women). Christians may honestly disagree over the meaning of 1 Corinthians 11. Regardless of how we interpret it, the matter is not central to salvation, but peripheral.

1 Corinthians 11:17-34—Why do Catholics believe the bread and wine actually turn into Jesus' physical body and blood?

Today I visited the Catholic shrine of the Virgin Mary of Guadalupe in Mexico City, where Mass is frequently celebrated. Mass entails *transubstantiation*, a literal sacrifice of the body and blood of Christ in the form of the communion wafer and the wine. The sacrifice is offered by priests. Yet the New Testament teaches that Jesus cannot be sacrificed again because his death was "once for all" (Hebrews 9:12,26; 10:10). Moreover, in the New Testament, every member of the body of Christ is a priest (1 Peter 2:5,9; Revelation 1:6; 5:10).

Roman Catholics believe that communion, or the Eucharist, is a *re-presentation* of the sacrifice of Christ, whereas the Protestant position is that it is only a *representation*. When Jesus said during the Last Supper, "This is my body," it is hard to believe that he meant he had two bodies—one doing the talking, and one they were about to eat. Besides, he also said that the cup is the new covenant (1 Corinthians 11:25), yet advocates of transubstantiation don't claim the cup is literally transformed into a covenant. To claim a mystic transformation of the bread into the body of Christ, inwardly though not outwardly, requires an unwarranted leap of logic and faith.

1 Corinthians 12:13—What is the baptism in the Holy Spirit? Is it a "second blessing"?

Paul assumes that every Christian has been baptized in the Spirit. (See also Titus 3:5; John 3:5; Mark 1:8.) So this isn't a second conversion or blessing; rather, it is tantamount to conversion to Christ.

1 Corinthians 13:1—In New Testament times, did people actually speak in angelic languages?

Paul did not say that the Corinthians spoke in angelic languages, only (hyperbolically) that even if they did, without love they would be nothing. He follows this with other hyperboles that refer to omniscience, to faith that literally moves mountains, and to extreme sacrifice. The later items in the series are not to be taken literally, so we have no logical or grammatical reason to take the first literally. The apostle continues to reason that uninterpreted languages are of little benefit and remain a mystery to all who do not understand, though never to God (14:2,5,13,19). I believe that New Testament languages (*tongues* in the Elizabethan English) were actual human languages (Acts 2:6-11; 1 Corinthians 14:10-11).

A few groups teach that speaking in tongues is evidence that someone has been filled with the Spirit, saved, or baptized in the Spirit. This is problematic. People were often converted and/or filled with the Spirit in Acts without mention of speaking in tongues (2:41; 4:4,8,31; 5:14; 6:3,5,7; 7:55; 8:36; 9:17,42; and so on). John the Baptist was filled with the Spirit from birth (Luke 1:15), yet he never performed any miracles (John 10:41). Being filled with the Spirit means being spiritual, allowing God to fill our hearts. Finally, Jesus Christ, as far as we know, never spoke in other languages—and he is our model.

1 Corinthians 13:8-13—What is the perfect thing that Paul anticipated?

To teleion might be translated six ways: the perfect, perfection, the mature, maturity, the complete, or completion. Many Bible readers understand this passage to refer to the second coming of Christ. The gender of the Greek construction is not significant in this case. The neuter noun (perfection) could refer to the state of affairs that will be reached in heaven, and this is a natural way of reading the passage. (But is it correct?)

Does this refer to the canon? The argument that "the perfect law that gives freedom" (James 1:25) is the New Testament is obviously flawed, since James is one *of* the New Testament documents—and an early one at that—and thus cannot be referring to the completed canon. Yet nearly all conservative interpreters concede that we no longer live in the apostolic era. Could the apostles' complete teaching be the perfect thing Paul had in mind?

Knowing fully or in part does not have to do with omniscience, but with the completeness of God's revelation. We will not have all knowledge even in heaven, for God alone is omniscient. Paul's argument seems to be that when his revelation is complete, we will no longer need prophetic gifts. Prophecy was a necessary filler during the apostolic period time. Most churches had few if any New Testament documents, and the apostles could not be everywhere at once.

Verse 13 may support this view that Paul is speaking of the second coming, depending on how "now" is understood. If the "now" is logical, we receive no help. If it is chronological, however, heaven is not in view, since presumably faith and hope would no longer be required, only love.

Ephesians 4:11-13 parallels 1 Corinthians 13:8-13. If the apostles are no longer with us, we have reached the "maturity" envisioned by Ephesians 4:11-16. (Not to say we don't have to continually strive to live up to the new reality.) The New Testament apostles and prophets (Ephesians 2:20; 3:5) ministered in the foundational stage of the Christian church. This is a time to which we will never return. Once the church had moved from its infancy into adulthood, minor gifts like languages, prophecy, and healing were to drop away, no more necessary than scaffolding for a building whose construction is complete. If this is the case, then whatever 1 Corinthians 13:10 is referring to as perfection, it is in the past. I think the view that the apostle is foretelling the maturation of the church through the apostolic age, including the completion of the canon, has much in its favor.

1 Corinthians 14:15—What is singing with the spirit?

Some think Paul accepts two varieties of Christian singing, one with the mind, and one with the Spirit. But there is another way to look at the passage. The Corinthians' problem was that they were being carried away by their feelings (1 Corinthians 12:2), a problem made even worse by ego and partisanship (1:10-17; 13:1-8). Paul is urging the Corinthians to think about what they are doing. Singing, like praying, involves the spirit and the mind. To sing in the spirit is to sing spiritually. See also "What is praying in the Spirit?" on page 236.

1 Corinthians 14:34-35—Should women remain silent in church?

First, we know that Paul never envisioned complete silence because earlier he mentioned women praying and prophesying (11:5). Second, the context of the passage has to do with weighing prophetic messages (see also 1 Thessalonians 5:19-22). If men and women were seated separately in the house churches, it would be awkward for couples to enter into a dispute on the meaning of a prophecy. Better to wait till afterward, when they are home. By the way, no manuscript lacks this passage, although in some manuscripts it comes after verse 40, so we can't simply ignore it.[13]

The sister passage is 1 Timothy 2:12, where Paul forbids women to have authority over men in the church. Some say Paul was so restrictive only because he was a man of his time, but there is a problem with this claim. In pagan religion, women often held positions of authority over men (as priestesses or prophetesses), and especially in Ephesus, the city to which 1 Timothy was sent. Paul's attenuation of the leadership role of women is thus not cultural, but countercultural. This is the historical understanding of the Christian church.

1 Corinthians 15:29—What is baptism for the dead?

This has to be one of the most problematic passages in the entire Bible. There are four or five main interpretations, though we will not take the time to go through them. The one interpretation that is *impossible* is the Mormon view—that you can be baptized for your ancestors to provide them an opportunity to respond to the gospel postmortem. There is no trace of such a practice in the New Testament or early Christianity. Colossians 2:12 teaches that only our own faith enables us to be saved.

Keep in mind that 1 Corinthians 15 is a chapter on the resurrection, a doctrine some teachers in Corinth were challenging. If there is no resurrection of the body, the dead will never make it to heaven. Paul insists that we are ultimately in a hopeless condition if our bodies are not going to be raised. Whatever view we settle on, it needs to make sense in the flow of Paul's thought.

Paul is making an ad hoc argument, not explicitly condoning baptism for the dead. An analogy may help. Once I was in Bulgaria, in a traditional church building where worshippers were lighting candles for the dead. If I later met one of these persons on the street, struck up a conversation, and found out he didn't even believe in life after death, might I not say, "If there's no afterlife, why did you light a candle for the dead?" I wouldn't be condoning this practice. In the same way, whatever the baptism for the dead means, Paul does not directly condone it. He only argues for the bodily resurrection of the dead.

1 Corinthians 15:50—What will our heavenly bodies be like? Will we retain our present injuries (Mark 9:43-47)?

Our bodies are crucial. We will not be disembodied spirits. We will be embodied—yet our bodies will not be like they are now. Our resurrection bodies will not be earthly, but heavenly. Flesh and blood will be transformed. Paul utilizes an analogy from botany (seed and plant). There is continuity between acorn and oak, yet also discontinuity. The difference between the two would never have been surmised based on the appearance of the acorn alone.

Consider Jesus' own resurrection body. As the firstfruits of the resurrection (verse 20), his body was renewed. Jesus walked on feet despite wounds inflicted only days before. The blood he had lost did not hamper his ability to function. So when Jesus speaks of entering heaven with one hand, one foot, or one eye, I understand him to be making a point about avoiding sin, not affirming anything about our resurrection bodies. There is no need to worry about missing teeth, hair, or other body parts. The resurrection body will not be defective.

1 Corinthians 16:19—Are house churches a viable option today?

The house church model seems to be more biblical than the model most of us are familiar with. That is not to say that church buildings, geographical leadership hierarchy, and formal services are unbiblical. Some challenges of the more informal model include leadership training, childcare, children, and organizational details when larger meetings are in view. Yet these obstacles are not insuperable. Perhaps small fellowships could join together monthly or quarterly with guest speakers or Bible teachers feeding the flock and stimulating discussion and study.

Most of the real personal growth in Christians' lives takes place in smaller groups through personal relationships. The early church met in homes for the first 200 years. New directions in the church can facilitate healthier dynamics.

2 Corinthians 1:13—Could most people write and read in the first century?

The apostle Paul clearly assumed a number of the Corinthians could read, but how many? Not everyone who could read could necessarily write, but a huge percentage of the free population had to read signs, inscriptions on coins, census material, and of course, bills, receipts, and tax information. The archaeological evidence is overwhelming. Professionals were often employed to write—even the learned Paul used a secretary (Romans 16:22)—but this does not indicate ignorance or illiteracy in the population at large.

First-century Palestinian Jews spoke Aramaic and were familiar with Hebrew (especially the priests and rabbis), and a number of citizens were also fluent in Greek—not to mention the Latin that some of the Roman soldiers and politicians must have known. It is fair to describe this society as trilingual.

2 Corinthians 5:10–When will we be judged, and when will we go to heaven?

Everyone on the planet, the quick and the dead, are judged at the same time (John 5:28-29). But how can this be true if the dead saints are already in heaven, as is affirmed at many funerals? Unless we postulate some sort of time warp, there must be a delay between death and judgment. That there is an intermediate state of the dead—which means that no one is in heaven or hell yet, as judgment will not take place until Christ returns—was the view of the ancient church.

Final judgment is *declarative*, not *investigative*. God won't examine the records of our lives, in something resembling a courtroom scene, to determine whether we will enter heaven. Rather, he'll declare what we knew from the moment we died and went to Hades: our final destiny. At this point the righteous will be escorted into the glory of heaven, and the wicked will be cast into the fire. In Daniel 7:10 and Revelation 20:12, where "the books were opened," the message is that God's sentence is just, not that he had to search the records in order to decide what judgment to render.

Christians are saved through Christ, so when we stand before the judgment bar of Christ, the Lord will review our lives and let us know about our coming reward, or "treasure in heaven," as Jesus taught. The notion of degrees of reward in heaven makes many uncomfortable. Yet we know that the more we put into something, the more we get out of it. If we exert ourselves strenuously in sports, the victory is sweeter than if we only gave 80 percent. A little extra reward awaits those who truly went the distance.

Christians are to live a God-fearing life, but we are not to live in dread of damnation or to be unsure of whether we have measured up. If we do the will of the Father, obeying his word, the last day will bring no rude shocks (Matthew 7:21-27). See further comments on Luke 16:23 and John 14:3.

2 Corinthians 5:21—Why did Jesus come to earth?

Jesus came to reconcile man to God and to preach about this great news. In a word, his visit to our planet was about salvation. This salvation is not just from the punishment we deserve for our sins, but also from the "corrupt generation" we live in (Acts 2:40; 2 Peter 1:3-4). To say Jesus came merely to improve our society is to omit the number one improvement we need—salvation.

Jesus came to reconcile us to God, and this hefty theme is constantly emphasized in the New Testament (Matthew 1:21; 20:28; 26:28; and many, many others). The implication of these passages is clear: Jesus' followers are to assume the same mission with the same urgency.

2 Corinthians 12:2—What is the third heaven? And is Paul referring to himself?

The ancient Jews thought of three heavens: the sky (the locus of the birds and clouds), the celestial heavens (the locus of the stars), and the third heaven (the locus of God and his angels). According to this interpretation, the third heaven is the highest heaven to which man can ascend. Some believed in many more heavens, though this goes beyond the Scriptures.

Some early Christians thought of this third heaven, or paradise, as contained in Hades, or the realm of the dead. Wherever it was, it was wonderful. And yes, the man is apparently Paul himself, given his modesty and reluctance to go into detail about the experience—which was, after all, ineffable. This stood in contrast to the snobbery of his opponents (2 Corinthians 11:12-15; Colossians 2:18-19).

12

Galatians to Philemon

Galatians 1:8-9—Why aren't the Gospel of Thomas and the Didache in the New Testament?

The Didache (pronounced "did-ah-KHAY," Greek for "teaching") is from around AD 100 and to a high degree reflects the thinking of the earliest Christians. However, it includes several elements at variance with biblical teaching. It was not included in the New Testament because not all its teaching is apostolic.

The Gospel of Thomas is a Gnostic work written much later—110 years after Matthew's Gospel, on which it depends. It would never have fit in the New Testament because much of the theology is skewed. Galatians 1 warns us that no one can change the gospel. The New Testament isn't missing any books because nothing was removed or lost. Quite simply, the early church did not recognize the authority of the Gospel of Thomas, nor has the Christian church through history.

The Gospel of Thomas is increasingly popular these days, especially among people who would believe that the New Testament is not a complete or accurate record of what Jesus taught during his earthly ministry. This spurious document is not a Gospel at all because the Passion narrative is absent. Unlike the four canonical Gospels, the Gospel of Thomas is only a list of sayings. It has no connection with the apostle Thomas, who, according to tradition, spread the teachings of his Master in India and died there for the faith.

The theology of the book is Gnostic. Insight is more important than morality, spirit more real and significant than matter. Gnosticism is making a comeback in the New Age movement. This philosophy-religion appealed to the ego without requiring any real commitment. Here are a few of the better-known of the 114 sayings in the Gospel of Thomas:

- "Jesus said, 'Happy is the lion whom the man eats, so that the lion becomes a man; but woe to the man whom the lion eats, so that the man becomes lion!'" (saying 7).

- "Jesus said, 'Let not him who seeks desist until he finds. When he finds he will be troubled; when he is troubled he will marvel, and he will reign over the universe'" (saying 2).

- "A person cannot mount two horses or bend two bows, and a servant cannot serve two lords" (saying 47).

- "Jesus said, 'He who knows the All and has no need but of himself has need everywhere'" (saying 67).

- "Simon Peter said to them, 'Let Mary leave us, because women are not worthy of life.' Jesus said, 'Behold, I shall guide her so as to make her male, so that she may become a living spirit like you men. For every woman who makes herself male will enter the kingdom of heaven'" (sayings 113–114).

Galatians 3:7—If "those who believe are children of Abraham," are all Christians also Jews?

No. Yes, we are children of Abraham and daughters of Sarah (1 Peter 3:6), but Abraham and Sarah weren't actually Jews because they lived centuries before Moses received the Law! Jews are descendants of Jacob, whose 12 sons became the 12 tribes of Israel. (Recall that Jacob's other name was Israel.) Jews must be circumcised, obey the Sabbath, offer the specified agricultural and animal sacrifices, and so forth.

"Father Abraham" is father of all the faithful. (We do not refer to "Father Jacob.") "The Israel of God" (Galatians 6:16) may refer to ethnic Jews who accepted the Messiah, Jesus. Yet even though the new covenant is best comprehended in the light of the old, that does not qualify us as Jewish.

Galatians 3:28—If there is neither male nor female in Christ Jesus, why should gender matter in marriage?

The Bible rejects homosexuality (see the comments on Romans 1:26-27), so gay marriage is clearly outside God's design. As for Galatians 3, the passage emphasizes our fundamental unity in Christ regardless of economic differences, religious heritage, or gender. It doesn't tell us that God has erased the distinctions! Slaves who converted were still slaves; Jews didn't stop being Jewish just because they were baptized; males were still male, females were still female, and God's beautiful plan for marriage (Genesis 2:24) was still intact.

Galatians 4:6—Why should Christians say "Abba"?

The Aramaic word for father, *Abbá,* reflects the language of the Lord's Prayer (the "Our Father" of Matthew 6:9-13). The word occurs three times in the New Testament (Mark 14:36; Romans 8:15; Galatians 4:6). The point is not so much to say this Aramaic word as to pray intimately to God as a loving father.

Galatians 5:18—What does it mean to be led by the Spirit? Will God always tell me what to do?

No, not really. Being led by the Spirit, here and in the parallel passage, Romans 8:14, means living by God's moral will in our lives (See also Psalm 143:10.). It does not mean receiving mystical instructions about where to go. The opposite of being led by the Spirit is living by the flesh. The Holy Spirit is less like a GPS for our lives and more like a moral compass. When we are living well, we enjoy the freedom to make our own decisions.

My experience runs counter to the supposition of some books on the subject. The longer I have been a Christian, the less the Lord has told me what to do. In the same way that we gradually let our children go, permitting them to make their own decisions, so the Lord entrusts us with increasing degrees of freedom.

Ephesians 1:1—Who are the saints?

The saints (Greek: *hoi hagioi*) are Christians! Along with *brother, believer,* and other terms, *saint* was a common appellation for any follower of Christ. In time, with the rise of the veneration of individual saints, the definition changed. Those who had given their lives for the cause were accorded special honor (understandably), and the term soon became reserved for the martyrs and other righteous persons. Soon it was seldom applied to believers in general—a biblical truth obscured. The saints are those who heard Paul's letter to the Ephesians read aloud. Anyone seriously trying to live a Christian life is a saint.

Ephesians 1:23; 5:32—The church is the body of Christ as well as Jesus' bride, so did Jesus marry himself?

Mixing two analogies (head/body and groom/bride) creates a strange brew. One is an organic illustration, the other a marital one. The head does not marry the body, and the bride is not the groom's body (even if in marriage they become one). Analogies only illustrate; they can't be creatively blended to yield new theologies. (Not true ones at any rate!)

Ephesians 3:21—Why is the church necessary? Can't I be a Christian without the church?

The church was Jesus' plan A. Apparently he expected his followers to continue to band together after his mission was accomplished. *Ekklesia* (church) appears 217 times in the Greek Bible by my count, including 3 times in Matthew (16:18; 18:17 [twice]). It means "assembly" and is the same word as in Acts 19:32,39-40. It wasn't a religious word per se.

The church helps us fulfill our basic spiritual needs for instruction, direction, worship, transcendence, and relationships. The church is the body of Christ (Romans 12:4-5; 1 Corinthians 12:12-27; Ephesians 1:22-23), so being in Christ is organically bound up with our Christian relationships. If you have been disillusioned with the church for whatever reason, consider Ephesians 3:20: "Now to him who is able to do immeasurably more than all we ask or imagine, according to his power that is at work within us, to him be glory *in the church and in Christ Jesus* throughout all generations, for ever and ever! Amen." Christ and his church go together; you don't have one without the other.

Ephesians 6:5-8—Should slaves be discouraged from escaping from abusive masters?

The consistent teaching of the New Testament is that we are *not* to oppose evil with evil (Romans 12:17-21). Accordingly, violent revolts would be difficult to justify. But violence isn't the only option. For example, the Hebrews' exodus from Egypt was not a revolt. The Lord personally and directly opposed the Egyptians; the slaves did not commit acts of violence themselves.

Now revolt is one thing; purchasing one's freedom is another. Paul told slaves in 1 Corinthians 7:21 to gain their freedom if they could. Further, the Old Testament stipulated that a runaway should not be returned to his master (Deuteronomy 23:15). God has a heart for the oppressed. The Bible has strong words of condemnation for slave traders (1 Timothy 1:10). But violence, murder, and other forms of payback are also precluded for the follower of Christ. Hoping for freedom and peacefully working toward that end are both good. Taking the law into our own hands is not. For more, see the entry on slavery (page 85).

Philippians 3:8—Is the Greek word for *rubbish* considered profanity?

Skubalon (possibly derived from *to tois kusi ballomenon*, "that which is thrown to the dogs") means dung, muck, scraps, or refuse. Paul also wrote Ephesians 4:29 and 5:3-4, so he did not sanction profanity, even if the first definition is in mind.

The Lord looks at the intentions of the heart. Still, Jesus said, "I tell you that men will have to give account on the day of judgment for every careless word they have spoken" (Matthew 12:36).

Philippians 3:20—As citizens of heaven, are we free to pledge allegiance to our nation?

The New Testament encourages good citizenship (Romans 13:1-2; 1 Timothy 2:1-3; 1 Peter 2:13-17). Of course, we are not to vow greater loyalty to the state than to God. The respect we render to our governing officials is different from and subservient to the reverence we offer to God (Matthew 22:21; Romans 13:7; 2 Peter 2:17).

Philippians 4:5—Is Jesus' second coming imminent?

Many first-century Christians expected Jesus to return soon. Yet some New Testament passages imply the opposite. Ephesians 3:21 speaks of "all generations," and the pastoral epistles discuss a long-term leadership plan (1 Timothy 3:1-13; Titus 1:5-9). Both are valid perspectives; we are to be ready at all times for the return of the Lord, *and* we are to prepare for a long winter before the renewal of all things. As Paul urges in 1 and 2 Thessalonians, we should settle down and live responsibly, not becoming distracted by speculations about the end of the world (1 Thessalonians 4:13–5:11; 2 Thessalonians 3:6-12). At the same time, we need to get ready, stay ready, and get others ready for the great and glorious coming of our Lord, with the prayer on our lips, "Come, O Lord" (1 Corinthians 16:22).

Colossians 1:6,23—Did the first-century church really preach the gospel all over the world and to every creature under heaven?

In Acts 2, Luke records the presence of Jews from around the Mediterranean world who had made the pilgrimage to Jerusalem for Pentecost (the Feast of Weeks), as the Old Testament required (Exodus 34:22-23). Luke is painting a picture of a highly international group. "Every creature under heaven" is a figure of speech—only 12 or 15 nations can be accounted for.

When people say, "I've traveled all over the world," this doesn't necessarily mean they have visited every country. It merely underscores the breadth of their travels; it paints a picture. The Bible commonly uses universal language to describe impressive (though less than global) activities or phenomena. Genesis 41:57 reads, "And all the countries came to Egypt to buy grain from Joseph, because the famine was severe in all the world." (See also Deuteronomy 2:25.) Did the denizens of South America cross the ocean to visit Egypt? Hardly. "All the countries" suggests that (1) the distribution of grain was no small operation, (2) those who came to purchase grain arrived from a number of directions and places, (3) the world seemed to be converging on Egypt (with Joseph as vizier over famine relief), and (4) God was bringing the Gentiles to his people, just as he would later intimate in such passages as Zechariah 8:23.

Paul does not mean that the entire world had been evangelized. In Colossians 4:5-6 he urges us to continue sharing our faith. The apostles and the following generation succeeded in evangelizing much of the Mediterranean world as well as parts of Asia and Africa, but southern Africa, Scandinavia, Australia, and the Americas remained unevangelized. The gospel did not reach China until around 500. It took nine and a half centuries before any form of Christianity reached Moscow. "Every creature under heaven" is a figure of speech. For one last and equally clear example, see Romans 10:18.

Colossians 4:14—Would Luke have been familiar with the Hippocratic Oath?

Hippocrates, the great ancient Greek physician, lived from 460 to 370 BC. As a physician, Luke would have been familiar with the oath.

The Hippocratic Oath is remarkable in several ways. It includes prohibitions against euthanasia, abortion, and breaches of confidentiality in the doctor-patient relationship. Further, no tuition fees are to be charged for medical training.

1 Thessalonians 4:13-17—When we die, will we "rest" (or "sleep") and then be awakened on judgment day? Or will we immediately be with God in heaven?

When we die, we do not go to heaven or hell; there is a waiting period between death and the judgment day. *Asleep* is not literal in this passage; it is a common metaphor for death. When we die, we go to "Abraham's bosom," or paradise (see Luke 16:22 NASB). As awesome as paradise will be, it is greatly inferior to what awaits us once Jesus returns, which is pictured as a room in the Father's home, a crown of glory, our eternal reward…(John 14:2; 1 Corinthians 9:25; Revelation 22:12). The Bible describes heaven in many different ways.

1 Thessalonians 5:1-2—Does the Bible tell us when Jesus will return?

Predicting the date of Jesus' return is fruitless. Scripture (Acts 1:7) and mankind's failed attempts throughout history make this clear. Those who predict the end of the world should be disregarded (though not the biblical message that we should be prepared for the end). A would-be prophet could get it right only out of sheer luck.

2 Thessalonians 2:3—Who is the man of lawlessness?

Many find in this passage a sort of antichrist—though the word is not used—whose rise presages the end of the world. Accordingly, such figures as Genghis Khan, Adolf Hitler, and Saddam Hussein have been nominated. After Paul's words in 2 Thessalonians 1:5-12, referring to the return of Christ, this interpretation seems reasonable. And yet it has a few problems.

- In 1 Thessalonians 5, Paul stresses the unpredictability of Jesus' return, whereas 2 Thessalonians 2 seems to point to a specific and somewhat predictable event.

- In Scripture, the coming of the Lord (verse 1) often indicates temporal judgments, not simply the last judgment. In Isaiah 19:1 and Micah 1:3, for example, the Lord comes against Egypt and Israel, respectively. Moreover, the day of the Lord (2 Thessalonians 2:2) is a time of punishment against Israel (Joel 2:1-2; Amos 5:18,20,27), not the entire world. Although universal and cosmic language is employed, the judgment is limited and relatively local.

- The Lord overthrows his enemies with the breath of his mouth (2 Thessalonians 2:8). See Isaiah 30:27-30 and Micah 1:3-5 to understand the metaphor.

- In Matthew 24:2-3,34, Jesus predicted his coming against the Jerusalem temple in his present generation. This took place in AD 70 through the agency of the Roman legions.

- The saints were to be gathered (Matthew 24:31; 2 Thessalonians 2:1) in Jesus and Paul's generation.

- The rebellion to take place beforehand (2 Thessalonians 2:3) naturally refers to the Jewish revolution against the Romans, the First Jewish War (AD 66–73).

- The man of lawlessness is therefore the Roman emperor. Caligula (AD 41–54) attempted to set up his ensigns in the temple but withdrew them. His successor, Nero (AD 54–68) didn't hold back, especially near the end of his reign during the Jewish War. Eventually Titus, the emperor-to-be who completed the destruction of Jerusalem (AD 70) defiled the temple with the imperial standards.

- Divinity was attributed to most Roman emperors, usually posthumously. Nero's claim to deity (verse 4) was audacious and directly conflicted with Christians' exclusive loyalty to Christ as sovereign. Nero was restrained in his earlier years, when his adoptive great-uncle, Claudius, still reigned and before his open brutality, preemptive assassination, and notorious perversity.

- The false signs (verse 9) of Roman religion are well known. Believers were not to be moved by them.

Though the preterist view—that the events Paul predicted took place through Nero (AD 54–68)—is logical and biblically defensible, it does not sit right with many thoughtful Bible students. All in all, both preterist and end-time interpretations have their merits. It is hard for most commentators (as for me) to commit completely to either alternative.

2 Thessalonians 2:9-11—Are present-day miracles counterfeit?

To challenge someone else's miraculous experiences is rarely productive, but we should evaluate them from a scriptural perspective. First, many answers to prayer are not wonders of biblical proportions. Second, sometimes those who do not know God perform impressive feats without necessarily being empowered by Satan. In Acts 19:13-16, we find the seven sons of Sceva exorcising demons. See also Deuteronomy 13:1-3. These supernatural actions are not ascribed to the demonic. Third, it is true that Satan can produce counterfeit miracles. They only imitate or approximate the real thing, as in 2 Thessalonians 2:9-11, yet who can distinguish the counterfeit from the genuine? Presumably only someone with expertise, with experience. We nonexperts may be fooled.

1 Timothy 2:15—In what way will women be saved through childbirth?

For the modern reader, 1 Timothy 2:15 is a strange verse. Paul can't be saying that a woman can live a godless life and automatically go to heaven if she has children. It is essential to know something about the false teachings Paul is addressing. He is instructing Timothy to combat Gnosticism, which held that the creator god was immoral, the body evil, and sex unclean. Many advocated celibacy, forbade marriage, and prohibited the consumption of various foods (1 Timothy 4:1-5). The Gnostics thought that childbirth made one unclean, but Paul insists that having children will not prevent Christian women from being saved.

1 Timothy 3:2—What does "the husband of but one wife" mean?

The Greek phrase "a one-woman man" has been interpreted three ways, as referring to polygamy, remarriage after divorce or the death of one's spouse, and marital faithfulness. Yet polygamy was rare in the Roman Empire in the first century, though not unheard of. Serial marriages were more common among the Romans, as well as among Jews who took a liberal view of divorce. Divorce was more common among the Jews of the first century, especially as liberal rabbis held that the "indecent thing" of Deuteronomy 24:1 could be that a wife burned the dinner or wasn't pretty enough for her husband! More conservative rabbis took the indecency to be adultery or another serious offense. Certainly divorce is a marital failure, but it's not clear to me why this would disqualify a man from ever serving as a church leader, especially if the fault lay with his spouse. The third view has the most going for it.

A one-woman man is simply someone who is faithful to his wife. It is the same construction used of the widow in 1 Timothy 5:9. (It would not make sense for her to be disqualified from church support for having lost more than one husband, nor would she be a candidate if one of her husbands was still alive. The "one-man woman" refers to the integrity of the widow: She had been faithful to her spouse.) Marital fidelity is required of church leaders. For more on eldership, see comments on Titus 1:6.

1 Timothy 4:10—In what way is God the Savior of all men? Will everyone be saved?

Jesus is described in Scripture as the Savior of the world (John 3:17; 4:42; 12:47). This refers to his ability, not mankind's actual experience. He is Savior only of those who are willing. God will not force himself on others, though he does desire that all would come to a knowledge of the truth (1 Timothy 2:3-4). Universalists believe everyone is already saved, but this requires a liberal biblical interpretation.

1 Timothy 3:2-3—Did Paul prohibit elders from drinking alcohol?

Paul writes that elders must be *nephalios* (sober, or temperate in the NIV) and not given to being *paroinos* (drunken).

Tragically, alcoholic consumption has wrecked millions of lives, but so have many things which, correctly handled, are benign or even positive in their effect: electricity, airplanes, painkillers, television… All can be abused, but this is a weak argument for forbidding them. Drunkenness is unacceptable for a follower of God (Proverbs 20:1; 23:29-35; Luke 12:45; 21:34; Romans 13:12-14; 1 Corinthians 5:11; Galatians 5:21; Ephesians 5:18; Titus 1:7; 1 Peter 4:3-4). However, consumption of alcoholic beverages in moderation is not a sin. Even Jesus was criticized for this.

I have studied the arguments on both sides—teetotalism as well as moderation. I respect those who advance the arguments, but the arguments themselves are less worthy of admiration. We all must be convinced in our own minds and not force our opinions on others. Romans 14:1–15:7 and 1 Corinthians 8:1–11:1 teach that we should not cause others to *stumble* and fall away from the Lord. They don't apply to those who are determined to *grumble*. Paul is warning us about violating others' conscience, not their opinion.

What about you? Do you ever drink too much? One of the dangers of alcohol is the impairment of judgment—not only your ability to drive a car but also your ability to make sensible decisions and conduct relationships in a selfless and godly manner.

1 Timothy 5:9—How long did people live in Bible times?

Life expectancy was shorter than it is today. Yet widows were ineligible to receive church benevolence until they were 60. A millennium earlier, the psalmist noted that some reached the age of 70 or even 80 (Psalm 90:10). With higher infant mortality, average longevity was significantly lower, yet for those who survived childhood (and childbirth), life spans exceeded those of some countries in the modern world.

1 Timothy 6:8-10,17—Is it a sin to be rich?

According to the Bible, being wealthy isn't a sin, but it brings great responsibility and can be hazardous to your spiritual health. The rich are warned of the perils and commanded to be generous toward others. For more, see the comments on Acts 4:32-37.

2 Timothy 3:8—Who were Jannes and Jambres?

According to an apocryphal Jewish tradition, these men were Pharaoh's chief magicians who attempted to simulate the wonders wrought by Moses.

2 Timothy 3:16-17—Is the New Testament inspired even though it wasn't complete when this verse was written?

This passage refers to the Old Testament, as do verses 14 and 15. Paul wrote 2 Timothy in AD 64–68, before most of the New Testament was written. But we can apply the passage to the New Testament by extension of the principle. First Timothy 5:18 refers to Luke 10:7 as Scripture (unless this was an independently circulating saying). Jesus himself hinted that more Scripture would come through the apostolic ministry after his departure (John 14:26; 16:13). Peter referred to Paul's letters as Scripture (2 Peter 3:16). The apostles and their immediate disciples wrote the entire New Testament.

2 Timothy 4:20—If Paul had the gift of healing, why did he leave Trophimus sick at Miletus?

In apostolic times, those with the gift of healing were not always able to exercise it, and not necessarily because of others' lack of faith, as in Matthew 13:58. Paul and Timothy also struggled with ailments (2 Corinthians 12:7-9; 1 Timothy 5:23).

Titus 1:6—Are people with unbelieving children disqualified from being elders?

The doctrine that elders' children must be Christians hinges on a narrow reading of a single verse—and one that can be translated two different ways. Even under the stricter view, the Bible does not specify whether every child must be a disciple (yet), it doesn't discuss the implications of a child leaving the Lord later in life, and it doesn't deal with exceptions or mitigating circumstances.

The other translation of the Greek *pista* (believing) refers to the children's attitude toward parents. This understanding seems to underlie many of the older translations. When the children mind their elders, showing proper respect, the prospective leader has done a good job in parenting, thereby gaining the knowledge of building family that is integral to church leadership. Either way, the fundamental point is obvious: Family experience and pastoral ability are organically connected.

Titus 1:12—How can Paul say that everyone from Crete is a liar?

In quoting a well-known Cretan writer, Epimenides of Knossos (sixth century BC), Paul is generalizing, not ruling out exceptions. If Epimenides' statement is literal, not intended as a generalization, it would be self-refuting, for in that case the poet himself would be lying! The churches among which Titus is ministering have presumably foresworn lying. The troublemakers of Titus 1 are sliding into the cultural sins of deceit and gluttony.

If this is offensive, consider the stereotype of the citizens of my homeland: loud, uncultured, overweight, ignorant of other cultures, constantly commenting on what things cost, and implying that other countries should imitate America. Embarrassingly, the reputation is often deserved, but it certainly doesn't fit every American.

Philemon 12—Why didn't Paul require Onesimus to repent and make restitution?

Onesimus ran away from Philemon, became acquainted with Paul in Rome, and was converted. Paul sent Onesimus back to his master (ignoring the law of Deuteronomy 23:15), presumably bearing a letter to the church that met in Philemon's home.

A window is thus opened into the New Testament doctrine of repentance. Surely it would have been spiritually beneficial for Onesimus to reconcile with his (former) master, confess wrongdoing, and make redress. But Paul allowed this to take place *after* Onesimus became a brother in Christ. Repentance isn't the sum total of actions issuing *from* the decision to follow Christ. Repentance is the decision itself. It is demonstrated in the deeds that follow (Luke 3:8; Acts 26:20).

13

Hebrews to Revelation

Hebrews 4:12—What's the difference between soul and spirit? Is this a reference to the human spirit or the Holy Spirit?

In the Bible, *soul* refers to the entire person (body and spirit), *spirit* to the spiritual part of the individual. We moderns may be tempted to impose our own categories of thought on biblical concepts and terminology. Specifically, we may conceive of soul and spirit as separate interior elements of human beings. When I was a small child, I believed that when we die, our souls leave our bodies. In the Old Testament, *nephesh* includes the body. Even in older English usage, one might say of a shipwreck, "all were souls lost." You may also remember that in the older English versions of the parable of the rich fool (Luke 12), the materialistic fool speaks to himself, "Soul, you have plenty of good things."

In mainstream biblical thought, soul is not a part of the person; it *is* the person. The spirit, on the other hand, is something interior and perhaps immaterial. (Recall that *spirit* in the biblical languages also can mean "breath.") Spirit was not conceived as something imaginary, but something very real, even if hidden from sight.

In Hebrews 4:12, *spirit* refers to the human spirit. The sword penetrates the heart, dividing (human) soul from (human) spirit. To divide soul and spirit, then, means to distinguish the spiritual aspect of a person (spirit) from the whole person (soul). In 1 Thessalonians 5:23, spirit, soul, and body are not three parts of a person. Rather, they refer to the person in three different aspects.

Hebrews 6:4-6—Are those who fall away incapable of being saved?

The Bible distinguishes between those who wander away (James 5:19) and those who fall away (Hebrews 6:4). Those in the first category have hope; those in the second do not. In light of Hebrews 6, perhaps it would be clearer to state that if they come back to Christ, they had not yet crossed the point of no return (Proverbs 29:1; Hebrews 10:26-31). Incidentally, when Matthew and Mark record Jesus' prediction that his apostles would all fall away on the night of his arrest, they used a different verb from that normally used for *falling* or *falling away*. (The verb in connection with these predictions is consistently translated "be offended" in the King James Version.) Therefore, we must distinguish between stumbling and falling.

Hebrews 8:10-11—Does this passage say that we will no longer have to teach people the Bible because they'll already know the Lord?

Not at all. Hebrews 8 describes the difference between the old covenant, where people normally entered the covenant apart from their will (as babies), and the new covenant, where only as responsible, believing, repentant individuals do we begin our relationship with God. The problem of the Old Testament was that people struggled greatly with their commitment because their parents made their decision for them.

Jesus showed us a different way; no longer would we be born into the church. Your parents cannot decide for you (John 1:13).

I realize that in one sense we all benefit from Bible teaching and deeply need it—we don't know enough just because we know the Lord—but this isn't the subject of Hebrews 8. To summarize, in Judaism you had to be taught to know the Lord, because you knew nothing about him when you entered the covenant. In Christianity, on the other hand, one has been instructed beforehand. You know what you're getting into.

Hebrews 10:4—If Old Testament sacrifices didn't take away sins, how were people forgiven?

Their salvation must have been granted in another way, and I would like to offer an analogy.

Douglas owes Steven $10,000. Douglas can't afford the payment now, but he has a friend, Joshua, who is willing to help. Joshua tells Steven, "I promise to pay you the full amount Douglas owes you." Steven is happy (though the price is yet to be paid), and Douglas is very happy.

Here is the point: Even though the price has not yet been paid, the debtor is released from his debt on the basis of the word of the one who will pay. The Old Testament saints were saved through Jesus, whose future death was like a promissory note that was guaranteed to be paid in full. And because of the power and integrity of Jesus' word, these men and women of faith were released from their debt of sin. In this sense, they were looking forward to the Messiah (John 8:56; 1 Peter 1:10-12).

Hebrews 10:26-27—Can believers lose their salvation?

This passage is referring to people who have deliberately rejected the sacrifice of Christ. Verse 29 ("the blood of the covenant that sanctified him") and verse 30 ("The Lord will judge his people") show that the writer has covenant people in mind. A number of other passages in the epistle support this view (2:1-3; 3:12-14; 4:1,11; 6:4-6,11-12; 10:36; 12:14-15). Nevertheless, some scholars interpret this passage as guaranteeing permanent salvation to true believers without the possibility of defection. While agreeing with them on the issue of eternal security—that apostasy on the part of a child of God is impossible—Luther diverged on the issue of the inspiration of Hebrews. The Hebrew writer, said Luther, was indeed referring to believers, which was why he rejected Hebrews as an uninspired document. (At least Luther was consistent.) Hebrews 10:26 speaks of a point of no return reached by the one who has fallen away. Many scholars accept the possibility of apostasy, including I. Howard Marshall, Robert Shank, and Stephen Ashby.[14] What is the support for the opposite view? How do believers on the Calvinist side (that it's impossible to leave God's grace) deal with the Scriptures warning of the possibility of losing one's salvation? Passages enlisted in support of the Calvinist view can all be understood in a non-predestinarian way. Romans 8:28-39 assures us that nothing can separate us from the love of God, yet it is our responsibility to keep ourselves in God's love (Jude 21). John 10:28-29 is often cited as proof of the impossibility of losing one's salvation, yet once again these words do not rule out one's walking away, turning one's back on God (Luke 9:62). It is only impossible for *external* powers to drag away a disciple against his or her will. Second Peter 2:20-22 clinches the argument. These people have "escaped the corruption of the world" (vividly symbolized by vomit and mud) by knowing our Lord and Savior Jesus Christ, which is possible only by participating in the divine nature (2 Peter 1:4). It is tortuous to argue that this washing applies to a non-Christian.

Hebrews 12:1—Who are these witnesses? Are the dead observing us?

No, they are those who have completed the race ahead of us, specifically the "hall of fame of faith" of Hebrews 11. The dead do not observe the living. The text does not say the witnesses are in heaven. They bear witness through their lives of faith. The cheering crowd is a metaphor.

Hebrews 13:22-25—Who wrote Hebrews?

This letter, unlike all other New Testament letters, is anonymous. The style is slightly Pauline, suggesting the letter was penned by someone in Paul's sphere of influence. Yet the early church consistently admitted that only God knows who wrote Hebrews. If they had no clue, our guesses are not more likely to be on target. Scholars have suggested many possible authors: Barnabas, Luke, Mary, Priscilla, and others. The most popular choice in our generation is Apollos—a man with the education level evinced in Hebrews, as well as one steeped in the Alexandrian style of this epistle. But the bottom line is this: No one knows who wrote Hebrews.

James 2:20-26—In what way is a person justified by what he does? How does this fit with Romans 4?

This verse refers not to the point in time at which we are *initially* justified, but rather to *ongoing* justification. The Lord requires a correspondence between what we profess and what we do, between our walk and our talk. Jesus insisted on this many times (Matthew 7:21-23). Abraham was justified when he believed God (Genesis 15:6). His faith and his actions were working together, as James pointed out, at Moriah (Genesis 22:1-18). Stepping back and looking at the big picture, we cannot be saved by works, but we can't be saved without them either! This is an important biblical theme.

As for Romans 4, the views of Paul and James mesh nicely. Both insist on an active faith—not a dead faith, but one that gets up and does something! Abraham actively pursued God, leaving Ur and believing in God's promises. Of course, he fell short of God's perfect righteousness, but still he was faithful to the covenant. Similarly, James argues that we cannot only talk the talk, we must also walk the walk. No contradiction here.

Some scholars, however, find a disagreement where there is none. Luther was so disturbed that he decided to insert the word *alone* after *faith* in his 1522 translation of Romans 3:28. He even relegated James, along with three other New Testament books of which he disapproved, to an appendix. But the solution is not hard to understand: True faith always expresses itself in deeds. Or as James says, "faith without deeds is dead." Faith without deeds is not true faith. Neither Paul nor James is confused. Both wrote correctly—just from different angles.

1 Peter 2:4-5,9-10—Who are priests in the New Testament?

In Judaism, priests were appointed from the lineage of Levi and his descendant Aaron. They offered sacrifices and represented the people before God and God before the people. Under the new covenant, there is no priesthood as such because all believers function as priests (Revelation 5:10).

However, a division between the clergy and the laity eventually developed in the church. By AD 250, church leaders were called priests. The "priesthood of all believers" was disintegrating. Professional church workers (clergy, as opposed to laity) were expected to be closer to God, live saintly lives, and obey the Scriptures. They were players, and the people in the pews were spectators. This is not what Christ taught.

1 Peter 2:13-17—What are we to do when human authorities and God's word disagree?

Sometimes governments ask us to go against the word of God. In such cases we must decline to obey (Acts 5:29). Ironically, 1 Peter 2:13-17 is sometimes used to support violent action, but the letter on the whole calls us to behave differently than the world does (1:14; 2:11; 3:9; 4:4; 5:9)—which is sure to be interpreted as strange. For example, during the terrible years of 1861–1865, many Christians refused to kill their brothers.

1 Peter 3:19—Did Jesus preach in hell between the crucifixion and resurrection?

Jesus was not in hell, but Hades (the intermediate place of the dead, sometimes mistranslated as hell). During this first Easter weekend,

Jesus proclaimed a message in the underworld. This passage may refer to all the dead (see also 4:6), those who perished in the flood, or fallen angels; there are several common interpretations. The exact nature of this preaching continues to be a matter of debate.

2 Peter 2:1-3—Who are these false prophets?

In Old Testament times, true prophets were often vastly outnumbered by the false ones (850 to 1 in 1 Kings 18:19; 400 to 1 in 1 Kings 22:6-8). The apostle foresees a time in the Christian age when false prophets will contradict the faithful messengers of the word. Their motives are selfish yet subtle. In Romans 16:17-18 they speak persuasive words. In 2 Corinthians 11:14-15 they masquerade as apostles, just as Satan masquerades as an angel of light. In 2 Timothy 3:6 they infiltrate and manipulate.

2 Peter 2:4—If God immediately judged angels when they sinned, are humans the only beings who can be saved through Jesus?

The Greek text says the angels are in Tartarus, not hell (as the NIV points out in the footnote). Godless humans will also be detained before the day of judgment, yet already tasting the punishment to come. The phrase *elect angels* (1 Timothy 5:21) implies that the angels have already made their choice and now fall into two categories: elect angels and fallen angels. Salvation through Christ is for humans, though ultimately all reconciliation is effected through the cross (Colossians 1:20).

1 and 2 John—Why does John repeatedly emphasize Jesus coming in the flesh?

These letters were written to protect believers from the false teaching of Gnosticism (see 1 John 1:1-2; 4:2; 2 John 7-11). This growing threat to the nascent church denied that Jesus had come in the flesh (the Incarnation) and taught that the physical world was evil, spawned by an evil god. *Gnosis* is the Greek word for "knowledge," as in 1 Timothy 6:20.

1 John 5:13—If we know we have eternal life, why do we need to work out our salvation with fear and trembling (Philippians 2:12)?

Salvation is past, present, and future. Past: Jesus' death was ordained before the creation of the world (1 Peter 1:20). Present: We receive forgiveness and cleansing on an ongoing basis (1 John 1:6–2:2). Future: We must persevere in order to enter heaven (Hebrews 3:14). As for Philippians 2:12, the imperative is plural. We are to work out our salvation together, corporately, as the people of God. The body of Christ should give us even more confidence that we are right with the Lord (1 John 5:3,13).

1 John 5:16-17—What sin leads to death?

Sin separates us from God—an eternal consequence—though various sins have different levels of impact. Sin affects the way we relate to others and to ourselves (psychologically). Perhaps we cannot rank all sins by category and degree of severity, but it simply isn't true that all sins are equal. Rudeness and selfishness can damage a relationship, jealousy can destroy it, and murder can erase it completely.

The sin that leads to death is singular, not plural. There are not some sins that lead to death and others that are okay. As I understand things, a sin leading to death is a sin that one refuses to repent of (Proverbs 28:13). Taking into account the Gnosticism of the false teachers troubling John's churches, the mortal sin may be rejecting Jesus or refusing to back down from the heretical position that Jesus was not a real person.

All sin leads to death, but that is a process. James 1:13-15 does not say that when you give in to temptation, you are dead. That comes about only when sin is full-grown. It is vain to pray for God to forgive people who deep down do not care for him and his ways—who do not *want* to be forgiven. For more on this, see also Jeremiah 11:14 and 14:11. To sum up, a sin that leads to death is not one particular sin, but rather any serious sin that we refuse to relinquish. See also comments on Mark 3:29.

2 John 7—Who is John referring to as the antichrist?

According to the elder John, whoever does not acknowledge the Incarnation—that Jesus was fully human, that God came in the flesh—is the antichrist. In other words, the antichrist is not necessarily a single person. There are, in fact, many antichrists (1 John 2:18,22; 4:3). See comments on 2 Thessalonians 2:3.

3 John 7—Should church staff members be paid?

Missionaries were supported by the church, not by outsiders. That is the point of the passage. Financial support is due for preachers (Matthew 10:10; 1 Corinthians 9:3-14; 1 Timothy 5:17-18), though they sometimes had to support themselves (Acts 18:1-3). First Timothy 5:17 and 1 Peter 5:2 imply financial support for elders too. More interesting perhaps is the apparent lack of a professional clergy in the first place. Churches had central leadership groups. We find apostles and elders in Jerusalem, prophets and teachers in Antioch, elders in Ephesus. Some of these persons were supported by the church (locally or by their home church); others were not.

Pay the staff if they are church workers. Salary level is not scripturally specified. I would encourage every congregation provide hardworking staff with a fair wage.

Jude 14—Why does Jude quote an apocryphal book?

The book of Enoch is quoted verbatim in Jude. What does this mean? Here are the possibilities:

- Jude believed the portion of Enoch he was quoting was correct even though the rest of the work was not.

- Jude believed the entire book of Enoch was inspired, but he was wrong.

- Jude thought the entire book of Enoch was inspired, and the inclusion of Jude in the New Testament suggests he was right.

The New Testament is abounding in quotations from a number of ancient works, some by believers, some by nonbelievers. Paul's speech on Mars Hill to the Areopagus has at least five allusions to or citations of pagan writers. Would anyone consider Paul to believe that these writers were inspired? Unlikely. But the case of Jude is a little different because Enoch is not an unbeliever, but the Old Testament man of faith described briefly in Genesis 5 and also in Hebrews 11. Nevertheless, citation from an ancient work no more proves its inspiration than a preacher's quotation of a modern poem or song suggests he takes the whole work as infallible.

Enoch has survived in the ancient Ethiopic language (in 40 manuscripts—and in fact is included in the Ethiopian Old Testament) and fragmentarily in Aramaic, Greek, and Latin, so we don't have to guess what the author wrote. His doctrine shines through in the writing, and there is much to commend in the book of Enoch. However, being cited is no compelling reason for the entire work being included in the Bible.

Jude 20—What is praying in the Spirit?

Ephesians 6:18 and Jude 20 encourage us to pray in the Spirit. The most straightforward explanation is that this means praying spiritually. Some groups hold that praying in the Spirit entails praying in unknown languages. But 1 Corinthians 12:28-30 shows that this gift was possessed only by some, and it was the least important of all the gifts of the Spirit. In our hearts we know the difference between fleshly prayer and spiritual prayer. Some prayers are full of self-reliance; others are marked by God-reliance. See also "What is singing in the Spirit?" on page 205.

Revelation 1–22–Where do we fit in the timeline of the Apocalypse?

Revelation was not written as a timeline. Some expositors disagree, but their approach has opened the door for hundreds of predictions of the end of the world and will doubtless continue to do so. Revelation gives a timeless message of hope and perseverance to Christians persecuted in the first century. The flow of this prophecy (Revelation 1:3) is more theological than chronological. It contains many allusions to the last judgment and the eternal kingdom, but it is not arranged chronologically.

Where are we today? In one sense we are living *after* much of the book of Revelation—judgment has fallen on the Roman Empire, and the vindication of the saints has begun. Yet in another sense, genuine disciples of Christ continue to look ahead to his coming, his decisive intervention in human history. The curtain is yet to fall; the final judgment is yet to take place—which puts us *everywhere* in the book, for in every passage we hear the voice of the one who is the Lamb of God and the Lion of Judah.

Revelation 1:3–Why did Jesus say the time was near?

Second Thessalonians 1:8-10 and Hebrews 9:26-28 tie the return of Christ to the end of the world and the judgment. Revelation presents pictures of the judgment of God's enemies, the vindication of his saints, the punishment of the wicked, and the eternal reward of the righteous. Yet Revelation also has a historical context, and the "coming" of Jesus in this book was partially fulfilled in God's judgment against the Roman Empire through a series of plagues, wars, invasions, and internal foes.

In Daniel 8:26 the "distant future" is a span of less than four centuries (around 530 BC to 165 BC). Why should Revelation 1:1-3 refer to a span of 2000 years—more than six times as long? Revelation sheds light on the ultimate fate of the wicked and the reward of the saints. Yet it has a specific historical fulfillment. Disciples of Christ should live in a state of preparedness for the coming of the Lord, which could take place at any time. Yet for the persecuting Roman Empire, judgment day came many centuries ago.

Revelation 2–3—Do the seven churches represent eras of church history?

This *historicist* interpretation first appeared in the Middle Ages, and the Seventh Day Adventists and the Worldwide Church of God latched onto it. Most scholars do not subscribe to the notion that Revelation describes the church through the centuries, era by era. The eras include loss of passion, persecution, false doctrine, permissiveness, hypocrisy, missionary opportunity, and materialism, but such scenarios have characterized the church of *all* ages. The seven-part sequence is imaginary. Further, all seven of the churches existed in John's day.

In fact, in the Bible, the number seven is often symbolic: The seven churches of the province of Asia in Revelation 2–3 are representatives of the universal first-century church. They are not seven consecutive eras, nor does the text present them in any sort of sequence.

Revelation 3:20—Where does the Bible talk about the sinner's prayer?

Revelation 3:20 is often cited, though strictly speaking these words are addressed to believers, not unbelievers. Jesus pleaded with them— not to be converted, but to be earnest and repent (3:19), to allow him back into their lives. Their lukewarm commitment was a symptom of the materialism that had pushed the Lord out of their hearts. Revelation 2:4 is a similar passage.

Prayer in general is a natural response for anyone who turns to the Lord (Matthew 7:7-8), but leading someone in the sinner's prayer in particular is a modern practice, stemming from the United States around the year 1830. We must take care in our teaching to emphasize discipleship (Acts 2:36-38; Colossians 2:6-7) because receiving Christ (John 1:11-13) includes accepting him as Lord. Receiving Christ is also equivalent to accepting his word (John 12:47-48). We come to Christ on his terms, not ours.

Revelation 3:20 is a wonderful passage that reveals God's heart toward all people: He desires to dwell in us. The infinite God cares for his finite creatures.

Revelation 7:2-4—Will only 144,000 people be allowed into heaven?

This misunderstanding is based on an overly literal reading. This passage and Revelation 14:1-5 utilize the number 144,000 to refer to God's redeeming of his people. If we took the number literally, we would be obligated to take other elements of the passage literally. Look closely at Revelation 7:4 and 14:4. The redeemed are Jews (not from the tribe of Dan), males, and virgins. Unless you are a celibate Jewish male not descended from Dan, you have no eternal hope. Here is one symbolic interpretation: 144,000 is 12 (the number of organized religion) squared for emphasis, times 1000 (a large number, perhaps 10 [the number of man] raised to the power of 3 [the number of God]). It refers to the full number of the redeemed who will be in heaven.

Revelation 7:9—Is Christianity narrow-minded and exclusive?

Critics of Christianity say it is exclusive. Although truth does exclude error and contradiction, the Christian faith is expansively inclusive. This passage describes the ultimate vision of multitudes of men and women worshipping God—from every nation, tribe, people, and language.

Revelation 7:13-14—Where are the tribulation and the rapture mentioned in the Apocalypse?

Tribulation comes from the Latin *tribulatio*, which is a translation of the Greek *thlipsis* (oppression, affliction). In the Bible, *tribulation* usually refers to the pressures, trials, and suffering that God allows his followers to endure (John 16:33; Acts 11:19; 14:22; Romans 5:3-5;

12:12; 2 Corinthians 1:6; James 1:2-3; 1 Peter 1:6-7; 5:10). In Revelation 6–18, the persecutors of Christ's people (Rome) receive divine retribution, depicted as a series of plagues and other punishments that mirror the ten plagues against Egypt (Exodus 7–12). These depictions are popularly known as the tribulation, though in fact, in Revelation 7 the tribulation refers to the persecutions the Christians were undergoing, so this is a misnomer.

Rapture is from the Latin *rapire,* a translation of the Greek *harpadzesthai* (snatch) in 1 Thessalonians 4:17. Pretribulationism, which became popular in the mid-nineteenth century, proposes the following order of events:

- the rapture
- the judgment seat of Christ (for believers)
- the seven-year tribulation
- the second coming
- the millennial kingdom
- the "great white throne" judgment and lake of fire (for unbelievers)
- the eternal state (for believers)

But the prevalent interpretation before the mid-nineteenth century goes like this:

- tribulation (throughout our lives as believers)
- the second coming, which triggers the resurrection of the dead, the rapture of the living saints, and judgment for all
- either heaven or hell

In this second view, the book of Revelation provides timeless lessons on God's faithfulness and stern treatment of the church's persecutors.

But the immediate application has to do with punishments to fall on the idolatrous and persecuting Roman Empire, not a twenty-first-century cataclysm. As for the resurrection of the dead and the rapture of the righteous living, these are events we can bank on and look forward to with eager expectation. Yet no one knows when they will take place. For more, see the comments on Revelation 1–22.

Revelation 16:8-9—When people refuse to repent, does God harden their hearts, as he did Pharaoh's during the Exodus?

We do see parallels between the plagues of the Exodus and those recorded in Revelation. Neither Pharaoh with his magicians nor the enemies of God in Revelation repent, despite ample incentive. In neither situation does God contravene human free will, but he may harden his enemies' hearts in Revelation as he does in the Exodus. In fact, whenever we decide to harden our hearts, God facilitates the hardening. In theological terms, the hardening on God's part and our own hardening are concurrent. (See the comments on Exodus 7:13.)

Revelation 16:16—What is Armageddon, and how can we prepare for it?

Armageddon comes from the Hebrew *har-Megiddo* (hill or mountain of Megiddo). The battle of Armageddon is not necessarily a literal battle. Revelation is a book rich with symbolism, including some 500 allusions to the Old Testament. The general vicinity of Megiddo was a frequent battleground. What did Revelation 16:16 conjure up in the mind of the reader or listener familiar with Old Testament history? Warfare. A showdown. The earliest recorded battle of Armageddon took place nearly 4400 years ago, and dozens of battles have been fought in the region of Megiddo since that time. This makes Armageddon a natural symbol of warfare.

I do not view Armageddon in any literal sense, though it is true that one of the central messages of Revelation is that the forces of good will ultimately triumph over the forces of evil. And if this is not a literal battle, we have no way to prepare for it physically. Instead, both Testaments urge us always to be ready to meet God. Instead of stockpiling water, canned goods, and ammunition, as some survivalists do, the Lord's will is that we heap up righteousness and good deeds, sharing what we have with as many as possible.

Revelation 17:3-5—Is Babylon, the mother of prostitutes, a symbol of America?

The West may not be falling politically or militarily (yet), but it has begun to fall morally. According to Edward Gibbon (1737–1794), author of *The Decline and Fall of the Roman Empire,* five signs characterized Rome's decay:

1. increasing love of show and luxury (affluence)
2. widening gap between the very rich and the very poor
3. obsession with sex
4. freakishness in the arts, masquerading as originality
5. increased desire to be supported by the government

Not surprisingly, social critics have drawn parallels between ancient Rome and modern Western culture. America leads the world in resources and affluence, so she is an apt choice for the comparison. Nahum 3:4 compares another entity with a harlot—Nineveh. Israel herself was often described this way (Isaiah 1:21; Hosea 1:2; 3:1-3).

Revelation 19:11-16—Will Jesus return in violence?

The picture of Jesus in Revelation is strikingly different from the one we get in the Gospels. His divinity, power, and role as Judge are undisguised. This entire passage is colorful and literarily picturesque. In Revelation, Jesus is both Lamb of God and Lion of the tribe of Judah (5:5-6,12). There are two sides. As Paul put it, "Consider therefore the kindness and sternness of God" (Romans 11:22). Some of us gravitate toward the image of Christ as Judge, the agent of God's wrath; others prefer to think of him as Savior, gentle and patient. Both images are justifiable scripturally.

Too often we think of God as simply nice. Yet the God of the Bible is hardly nice. Kind, gracious, compassionate, and good he may be, but not inoffensive, insipid, or innocuous. In the same way, Jesus as Son of God isn't nice either. As others have said, he came to comfort the afflicted and to afflict the comfortable. Check out Luke 2:34; 24:19. Jesus' followers are not called to be nice, but to speak the truth in love (Ephesians 4:15,25).

Revelation 19 pictures Jesus dealing with the persecutors of the people of God. More broadly, at the judgment day, God will deal severely with those who reject him. Hebrews 4:12 also mentions a sword of judgment, though without the violent images of the Apocalypse. In Hebrews, the sword is simply the word of God (his truth, his message), not the Word of God (the Incarnate Son). Yet the two are closely connected (Revelation 1:16; 2:12,16; 19:15,21).

Revelation 20:1-6—What is the millennium?

Those who claim to take Revelation literally affirm a thousand-year reign, or *millennium* (Latin for 1000 years). A dispute centers round the timing of Jesus' second coming. Some say it will come *after* the millennium (post-millennialism). Others, the majority, put the second coming *before* the millennial rule (pre-millennialism). Still others deny that the numerical picture in Revelation 20 should be taken literally in the first place (a-millennialism—my own view).

Revelation is a book of symbols, including symbolic numbers (7 churches, 24 elders, 144,000 people in heaven). The image of Christ reigning for a millennium, having triumphed over Satan, represents the victory of the cross, as does the scene of the vanquishing of the red dragon in chapter 12. Apocalyptic literature was not intended to be interpreted literally. We ought rather to ask, "What does this picture mean?"

Revelation 20:7-8—Why does the Bible picture the world as flat?

The ancient Hebrews believed in a *firmament*, which is firm (Genesis 1:6 KJV). This is a hemispherical metal-like dome covering the disk (circle) of the earth. The earth is a disk (Isaiah 11:12; Revelation 7:1) orbited by the sun (James 1:11). But this is not a point of doctrine, nor are we required to believe everything the ancients held to. The early Greeks knew of the sphericity of the earth as early as the third century BC, but many in the church did not concede the point until a thousand years later. Christians also defended the geocentric model against the heliocentric theory until the seventeenth century. Modern battles continue to rage in the area of biology (specifically evolution). Yet as Galileo (1564–1642) said so well: "The Holy Spirit intended to teach us in the Bible how to go to heaven, not how the heavens go." The Bible does not incorrectly teach that the earth is flat—unless every incidental detail is viewed as a matter of doctrine. Unfortunately, some Christians fall into this flawed approach.

If the point of Scripture is to convey truth about God, why couldn't (or wouldn't) God use accommodative language to communicate with humans? As in the Incarnation, the Lord accommodates himself to our level. The ancient languages themselves served as mere vehicles for divine truth, and there was no need to correct the science of the day. God's agenda didn't include correcting ancient cosmology, explaining the minutiae of particle physics, or enriching the vocabularies of the Jews or Christians. You and I employ words like *sunrise* and *sunset*, so let's not get hung up on incidental matters. There is nothing silly about God revealing his word through the medium of contemporary categories of language and cosmology. In fact, this shows his wisdom.

Revelation 20:13—What does "death and Hades" mean?

Hades is the Greek god of the underworld, but *Hades* has another meaning: the underworld itself. The term has been adapted from the Greeks. The Bible teaches that after death but before the Lord's return to take us to be with him in heaven (John 14:3), the dead will wait in Hades. *Death* and *Hades* are synonyms in Revelation 20:13. Thanks to the cross, death no longer has ultimate power.

Revelation 22:14-15—Why do we see unsaved people in heaven?

The end of Revelation is doing more than alluding to the final judgment, heaven, and hell. This part of the Apocalypse refers to the church triumphant as it has been delivered from the persecutor (the Roman Empire). The presence of the unconverted suggests that this is not a definitive description of heaven.

Notes

1. For more on this, a thoroughly helpful work is Ronald L. Numbers, *The Creationists: The Evolution of Scientific Creationism* (Berkeley: University of California Press, 1992).

2. David Frost, *Billy Graham: Personal Thoughts of a Public Man* (Colorado Springs: Cook Communications, 1997), 72-74.

3. The Acworth Letters, Letter of December 9, 1944. Available online at www.asa3.org/ASA/PSCF/1996/PSCF3=96Ferngren.html.

4. Timothy Keller, *The Reason for God: Belief in an Age of Skepticism* (New York: Riverhead Books, 1997), 97, 275. Interestingly, Asa Gray, a Christian and professor of botany at Harvard, was Darwin's chief proponent in the United States. In a letter to James Dwight Dana, Darwin said, "No one person understands my views & has defended them so well as A. Gray—though he does not by any means go all the way with me." Another nineteenth-century Christian friend of evolutionary theory was Henry Drummond (1851–1897), a colleague of Dwight Moody. One final example of a firm Bible believer who accepted as brothers in faith those who hold to evolution is R.A. Torrey. He was associated with Moody Bible Church and served as editor of *The Fundamentals* (published 1910–1915). Torrey said it was possible

"to believe thoroughly in the infallibility of the Bible and still be an evolutionist of a certain type."

5. Carol A. Hill, "Making Sense of the Numbers of Genesis," *Perspectives on Science and Christian Faith*, volume 55, number 4, December 2003, 239-52.

6. Adapted from Davis A. Young, *The Biblical Flood: A Case Study of the Church's Response to Extrabiblical Evidence* (Grand Rapids: Eerdmans, 1995). Available online at www.bringyou.to/apologetics/p82.htm.

7. Sarah Zielinski, "Ready for Contact," *Smithsonian*, winter 2010, 48.

8. Abraham Joshua Heschel, *The Prophets* (Peabody, MA: Hendrickson, 1999), 16.

9. The classic work is Edward Fudge's *The Fire That Consumes* (iUniverse, 2000). The best known of other scholars is probably John Stott. See also David L. Edwards and John Stott, *Evangelical Essentials: A Liberal-Evangelical Dialogue* (Downers Grove: InterVarsity, 1988), 312-20; Clark Pinnock, "Fire, Then Nothing," *Christianity Today*, March 20, 1987, 40-41; John Wenham, *The Goodness of God* (London: InterVarsity, 1974), 27-41; Philip Hughes, *The True Image* (Grand Rapids: Eerdmans, 1989), 398; and Stephen Travis, *I Believe in the Second Coming of Jesus* (Grand Rapids: Eerdmans, 1982), 196-99.

10. All references are to the standard 10-volume edition of the Antenicene fathers. Thus Lactantius, 7.217 refers to the work cited of Lactantius in volume 7, page 217.

11. William Barclay, *Daily Study Bible Series: The Gospel of Luke*, revised edition (Philadelphia: Westminster/John Knox, 1975), 269-70.

12. David Van Biema, "Christians Wrong About Heaven, Says Bishop," *Time*, February 7, 2008. www.time.com/time/world/article/0,8599,1710844,00.html; "Randy Alcorn," *Christianbookpreviews.com*, www.christianbookpreviews.com/christian-book-author-interview.php?isbn=0842379428.

13. Whether we interpret these verses through a cultural lens or as a binding policy for our time, this "gynecological passage" is not an interpolation. If you want to go deeper, I recommend James Beck, *Two Views on Women in Ministry* (Grand Rapids: Zondervan, 2005).

14. I. Howard Marshall, *Kept by the Power of God: A Study of Perseverance and Falling Away* (Paternoster Press, 1995); Robert Shank, *Life in the Son: A Study of the Doctrine of Perseverance* (Bethany House, 1960); Stephen Ashby, in J. Matthew Pinson, ed., "A Reformed Arminian View," *Four Views on Eternal Security* (Grand Rapids: Zondervan, 2002).

Index

For more than 1000 questions and answers, as well as books, audio sets, and DVDs on a wide array of biblical topics (including church history, marriage and parenting, world religions, leadership, and Christian evidences), visit Doug Jacoby's website at

www.douglasjacoby.com

You'll Also Love These
Harvest House Books About the Bible

Why the Bible Matters
Mike Erre

Mike Erre, teaching pastor of a large, culturally relevant church in Southern California, offers intelligent
answers to questions emerging generations are asking
about the Bible. He upholds the Bible's authority in
creative, engaging, and intellectually satisfying ways.
Erre's contagious enthusiasm and deep respect for the
Scriptures match his first-rate scholarship.

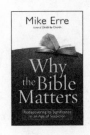

Knowing the Bible 101
Bruce Bickel and Stan Jantz

With extensive biblical knowledge and a contemporary perspective, Bruce Bickel and Stan Jantz provide
a manageable approach to understanding God's written message—its origin, themes, truth, and personal
relevance.

To learn more about Harvest House books and
to read sample chapters, log on to our website:

www.harvesthousepublishers.com

HARVEST HOUSE PUBLISHERS
EUGENE, OREGON